Lay Ministry Adviser

The Anglican Understanding
of the Church

Paul Avis is General Secretary of the Council for Christian Unity of the Church of England. Previously he was a parish priest in the Diocese of Exeter. As Prebendary and Sub Dean of Exeter Cathedral and Research Fellow in the Department of Theology of the University of Exeter, he serves as Director of the Centre for the Study of the Christian Church. He has been a member of the Church of England Doctrine Commission and vice-chairman of the Faith and Order Advisory Group and has served on the General Synod. Dr Avis' books include *Faith in the Fires of Criticism: Christianity in Modern Thought* (Darton, Longman & Todd, 1995) and *God and the Creative Imagination: Metaphor, Symbol and Myth in Religion and Theology* (Routledge, 1999). He is editor of *Divine Revelation* (Darton, Longman & Todd, 1997). He and his wife Susan have three strapping sons and live in South London and North Devon.

K1144/86

The Anglican Understanding of the Church

An Introduction

Paul Avis

First published in Great Britain in 2000 by
Society for Promoting Christian Knowledge
Holy Trinity Church
Marylebone Road
London NW1 4DU

British Library Cataloguing-in-Publication Data

A catalogue record for this book is available from the
British Library

ISBN 0-281-05282-4

Typeset by David Gregson Associates, Beccles, Suffolk
Printed in Malta by Interprint Ltd.

Contents

Preface

Until recently, Anglicans of the Church of England (though that is only a part of the worldwide Anglican Communion) were able to take their church for granted. Its pedigree went back long before the Reformation to the beginnings of Christianity in Britain and Ireland. It was the majority church, having baptized about half the population. It officiated at most funerals. It had its parish churches and clergy in every community. Its history was inextricably intertwined with the history of the nation. It was recognized by the state and connected to the crown. It had its chaplains in schools, colleges, hospitals, prisons and the armed services. Its worship and ministry was woven into the very fabric of the community.

All that is still true and needs to be reaffirmed, but it is much less secure. In some parts of the nation the position of the Church of England is tenuous. Though in many villages, market towns and affluent suburbs the parish church has a central role and an effective ministry, the work is becoming harder. Even in the inner cities, the parish church is still a significant presence, but its impact on local culture is marginal. Everywhere, however, the Church of England is under pressure from two modern phenomena that go under the catch-all names of secularization and pluralization.

The complex process that sociologists call *secularization* refers essentially to the diminished influence of religion on public life and on the common expressions of culture. Secularization does not necessarily mean that people generally are less religious or that prayer is not important to them or that they do not hold beliefs about sacred or transcendent meanings and values. But it points to the evident fact that religious beliefs and religious authority no longer figure prominently in many public institutions, such as Parliament, or in most expressions of cultural life, such as the media.

Secularization is related to privatization which refers to the way that religious beliefs, practices and values – marginalized in public discourse and community activities – are increasingly relegated to the personal and family contexts. Religious beliefs and commitments are not thought suitable candidates for public affirmation.

Let me take an example of secularization-privatization that will be familiar to everyone, at least in England and Wales. The decoupling some years ago of the Christian festival of Pentecost (Whitsun) from the Spring bank holiday (Whit Monday) and the resulting confusion in the minds even of churchgoers as to the date of Pentecost is a token of this process. The outcome is that Pentecost has become a second-class festival for the Church – which then has to work all the harder to make it meaningful. This example illustrates how practising Christians are increasingly not assisted by public institutions to observe their faith (secularization) but are compelled to observe it in their own time and for their own motives (privatization).

Alongside secularization stands the process (much more long-term) of *pluralization*. It is true that there has never been a time (certainly not since the Reformation, nearly half a millennium ago) when the Church of England had an absolute monopoly of the religious belief and practice of the population. There were always communities who did not identify with the national church (in Elizabeth I's reign, the so-called Separatists and recusant Roman Catholics; a century later, the Jews; since then, substantial communities of nonconformists). The theory was, however, that all members of the community ('commonwealth') were members of the Church of England and this principle undergirded the church's involvement in local, regional and national government, education, health care and supervision of moral behaviour.

Today, on the other hand, Anglicans in England are one faith community among others. They may be easily the largest in terms of nominal membership but they are not dominant. Their beliefs and values have to compete in the market-place of faiths, which includes non-Christian religions, such as Islam and Hinduism, as well as other Christian communities such as the Roman Catholics, Methodists and Baptists. While the relationship between the churches is generally excellent and practical co-operation is strong, the existence of a plurality of faiths has the effect of relativizing the claims of each.

Secularization and pluralization mean that as English Anglicans we can no longer take our church for granted. We know that our message will not be heard, our ministry will not be received, our values will not survive, unless we grasp the challenge of mission with both hands. To do that we need, among other things, an understanding of our message, our ministry, our values. The competitive situation in which as Anglicans in England we now find ourselves means that we cannot assume that people either inside or outside the church know what we stand for.

This brief introduction to the Anglican understanding of the Church is intended to meet this need. I hope it will be useful to students training for ordination and to the increasing numbers preparing for various forms of lay ministry, as well as to clergy who may have a nagging sense that their ordination training somehow forgot to tell them much about the Church itself and particularly about the Anglican expression of the Church. I hope that many lay synod members, churchwardens and Parochial Church Council members will want to read it. I want it to be useful to enquirers, whether they are wondering what the Anglican tradition has to offer in the market-place of faiths or whether they are preparing for a process of selection that may lead to training for a recognized form of ministry.

So far I have talked only about the Church of England. I needed to start from that point. But Anglicanism is a worldwide expression of the Christian Church. The other member churches of the Anglican Communion – 36 of them – are already familiar with the challenges that the Church of England is beginning to face. Their circumstances have generally been rather different from those of the Church of England. They are not usually majority churches. They are not established by law. They do not, in most cases, have centuries of history behind them. They are not, generally speaking, territorial churches in the same way as the Church of England is, with its parochial structure going back to Saxon times. They do not have substantial historical resources. Most Anglican churches have always had to pay their way and fight their corner. They are more aware than we English Anglicans of the need to know what we stand for, to be aware of what is distinctive about our doctrine of the Church. This introduction is meant for them too.

But there is another factor that challenges us to grapple with the doctrine of the Church and the Anglican tradition of interpreting that doctrine. Anglican self-awareness has been raised further by the ecumenical movement. As Christians from different traditions have come together in theological dialogue and practical co-operation – as centuries of suspicion and alienation have been broken down – they have all been compelled to ask: What do we stand for? How is our view of the Church distinctive? Where do we disagree with others? Where do our basic beliefs come from? Who decides and on what authority? Possibly, ecumenical engagement has proved more of a challenge to Anglicans than to members of some other traditions. I hope this book will assist the understanding of Anglicanism in situations of local ecumenism, such as Local Ecumenical Partnerships, and in the informal discussions and study groups that bring Christians of different denominations together, especially during Lent.

There are several introductions to the Anglican Communion, its structures and traditions, as opposed to Anglican theology of the Church. On Anglicanism generally there is a major textbook (to which I have contributed) with substantial theological material: *The Study of Anglicanism*, edited by Stephen Sykes, John Booty and Jonathan Knight (2nd edition, SPCK, 1998). But I am not aware of anything comparable on the Anglican understanding of the Church at this level and at this length.

I have tried not to make too many assumptions about the reader's previous knowledge. Those who want to study these matters further will find pointers to more advanced reading in the bibliography. I should add that I have not attempted to expound the range of Anglican theology of the ministry and sacraments, though obviously those topics are touched on. The subject is just too vast for this sort of book. What this book aims to provide, then, is an introduction to Anglican ecclesiology – in particular to its sources, spirit and shape. Our first task, then, is to explain this technical term 'ecclesiology'.

Before that, however, I need to make it clear that, as General Secretary of the Council for Christian Unity of the Church of England, I am writing in a personal capacity and not attempting to represent the views of the Council for Christian Unity. Nevertheless, I see myself as speaking from the mainstream of Anglicanism and as seeking to articulate a consensus on the Anglican understanding of the Church.

I am most grateful to Richard Bourne, my Research Assistant at the Centre for the Study of the Christian Church, for compiling the index for this book.

Paul Avis
Council for Christian Unity/Exeter Cathedral/Department of Theology, University of Exeter/Centre for the Study of the Christian Church

1

Why Christians Need an Understanding of the Church

The technical term for the study of the Christian Church is 'ecclesiology'. The word is made up of the Greek *ekklesia* (assembly) and *logos* (discourse) to stand for ordered speech about the Church – just as the word 'theology' is made up of the Greek *theos* (god or God) and *logos* (discourse) to stand for ordered speech about God and the things of God.

In its original meaning *ekklesia* is a secular term for an assembly of people and is derived from the verb to call. It was employed by those who translated the Old Testament (the Jewish Bible) from Hebrew into Greek before the coming of Christ. This version, known as the Septuagint (LXX), used *ekklesia* to translate the Hebrew *qahal* (assembly), which in turn derives from the Hebrew for voice (*qol*). Incidentally, the Septuagint also used *sunagoge* (cf. synagogue) to translate *qahal*. In both Hebrew and Greek, then, the Church is the assembly of those who are called – called together (to worship God) or called out (of the world, to serve him). It is worth noting in passing, however, that the English word 'church' (cf. Scottish 'kirk') comes from a different source: the Greek *kuriake*, 'belonging to the Lord (*kurios*)'.

The transition from the secular meaning, 'assembly', to the Christian meaning, 'church' in the theological sense, is found in the New Testament as well. *Ekklesia* is found in only one of the Gospels (Matthew), where it occurs three times. On two occasions it still has its basic meaning of 'assembly' (Matthew 18.17: 'tell it to the church'), but the third instance has the broader sense: 'on this rock I will build my church' (Matthew 16.18).

In the Epistles, *ekklesia* occurs frequently and three uses can be discerned.

⊚ First, there is the local Christian assembly or community: 'All the churches of Christ greet you,' writes Paul, apparently referring with some exaggeration to the scattered congregations in the various cities and towns of the Roman empire where he had planted churches during his missionary journeys, together (presumably) with other congregations founded by other Apostles, with whom they were in contact (Romans 16.16).

⊚ Second, there is the Church in general, the Church as such, the Church in a generic sense. 'I persecuted the church of God,' Paul confesses (Galatians 1.13), meaning the Church conceived as a single entity, wherever it may be found. Through his encounter with Christ on the Damascus road ('Why are you persecuting *me?*'), Saul (as he then was) had come to identify the community of Christians in Damascus with the totality of Christians, organized into communities.

⊚ Third, there emerges in the later Pauline and pseudo-Pauline Epistles a mystical or cosmic sense of *ekklesia* as the body of which Christ is the head (Colossians 1.18: 'He is the head of the body, the church'; Ephesians 1.22f: 'the church, which is his body, the fullness of him who fills all in all'). This usage seems to transcend the individual local congregations and even the whole Church on earth. It is this third sense which approximates most closely to the affirmation of the Niceno-Constantinopolitan Creed (the one used at the eucharist): 'I believe in ... one, holy, catholic and apostolic Church.'

Hans Küng, the leading contemporary Roman Catholic theologian, speaks of ecclesiology as the theological expression of the Church's image (cf. Küng, 1971). *The New Catholic Encyclopedia* defines ecclesiology in a nuanced way as 'the branch of theology that seeks to give a scientific exposition of the faith of the Church concerning itself'. Ecclesiology is, therefore, reasoned and informed reflection on the nature of the Christian Church.

Ecclesiology has a number of departments or sub-divisions: missiology; pastoral theology; the theology of the ministry and sacraments; worship and liturgy; structures of authority; ecumenical theology. Although ecclesiology clearly has a practical dimension and is nothing if it is not applied to the life of the Church, it is essentially a branch of Christian doctrine, concerned with what we believe about the Church and God's purpose for it and how that purpose is to be carried out in accordance with God's will revealed in scripture as interpreted in the light of tradition and reason. Therefore ecclesiology is not merely descriptive but has an inescapably prescriptive function. Ultimately it aims to say what the Church should be like and how it should carry out its mission. Ecclesiology is normally undertaken from a position of Christian belief and informed by commitment to the Christian Church.

Ecclesiology must certainly have a prophetic, critical dimension. It will not merely celebrate the Church's past glories – if at all – but will also sit in judgement on the failings and shortcomings of the Church in history and in the present. In this part of its work ecclesiology will draw not only on 'internal' sources of critique, such as the biblical prophetic books and the major reforming insights of historical theology (such as the Protestant Reformation and the theological renewal of the Second Vatican Council of the Roman Catholic Church, 1962–65), but also on historical and sociological studies of the Church as an empirical, worldly phenomenon that can be studied by secular disciplines.

Ecclesiology can also learn from secular traditions of critique, especially ideological criticism in the broadly Marxist tradition that helps to uncover the legitimation in ideas of material vested interests and oppressive distributions of power (for which critique the Christian Church is an obvious candidate).

Issues of authority, leadership, government and discipline particularly invite analysis and comment from the social sciences, and ecclesiology cannot afford to ignore this contribution, even though its comparative, relativistic and critical approach may seem threatening. Some classical ecclesiologies – Roman Catholic, Orthodox, Anglican, or Protestant – claim that the nature of the Church, including its structures of government or oversight, its outward political aspect or polity (papal, episcopalian, presbyterian or congregational) is given by God in divine revelation and is not subject to the judgement of human reason. They tend to assert that the ultimate integrity of the Church is guaranteed by divine providence, so that the vicissitudes of Christian history become retrospectively baptized as the unfolding of a divine purpose. The Roman Catholic Church officially holds that its teaching is not shaped by contingent cultural factors and that its papal and episcopal structure is ordained by God through Jesus' commissioning of Peter and the other eleven Apostles.

Similarly, some modern theologians in the tradition of Karl Barth (d. 1968) – John Milbank being a notable contemporary example – regard the social sciences as tendentious and reductionist in relation to Christian theology, rather than as offering ideologically neutral conceptual tools to help us understand the Church. They see no place for scrutinizing the Church and its structures by merely human methods that are not subordinated to divine revelation in scripture. This scepticism with regard to the likely ideological motives of ideological criticism itself is well taken, but any suggestion that the truth of God can be discerned and known in abstraction and isolation from cultural and socio-economic influences is no less ideologically naive. Christian truth is embedded in contingent human and social realities. Rare are the theologians, such as the great Protestant theologian F. D. E. Schleiermacher in the early nineteenth century, who can accept that the outward face of the Church in history – its political aspect, so to speak – is largely contingent but nevertheless hold that that fact does not detract from the abiding validity of the inward essence of Christianity. However, once we accept, in continuity with the dynamic of the Reformation, which saw the Church as continually reforming itself (*Ecclesia reformata semper reformanda*), that the critique of Christianity belongs to the very essence of Christianity, a cautious welcome is assured for the commentary offered by the social sciences.

The aspects of ideological critique that are particularly

relevant to ecclesiology concern the distribution of power and the exercise of authority in the Church (see Avis, 1992). This theme comes into focus in several areas: the bearing of particular political models – centralized and hierarchical (mon-archical) or dispersed and consultative (conciliar) – on church government and the relation of Church and state; the models of authority that pertain in the Church (traditional, bureaucratic or charismatic, to use the sociologist Max Weber's well-known typology); the ideological investment that established institu-tions make in the formulation and enforcement of official teaching ('dogma') which inevitably reflects sectional interests and refracts and distorts the interpretation of divine revelation; and the unmasking of gender bias and prejudice (sexism, androcentrism and patriarchy) in the Church in the light of feminist critiques (see Avis, 1989b).

Social science critique is not the only factor militating against the grandiose, absolutist and authoritarian ecclesiologies of the past. These were often dependent on equally grandiose, absolutist and authoritarian forms of 'secular' political struc-ture. Traditionally, Christianity has tended to uphold, both in its teaching and its discipline, the ideal of unanimity of belief and uniformity of practice (expressed, for example, in the various Acts of Uniformity that govern English religious history up to modern times). These ideals were thought to be demanded by the unity of God. This aspiration has actually belied the reality of diversity and conflict in the Church from New Testament times to the present day. The pluralism of faith and practice in the Church today mirrors the pluralism in society at large. Theological pluralism is a product not only of the creative fertility of the theological imagination, working on the resources of revelation in scripture and tradition, but also of the diversity of social and cultural settings in which theology is carried on, from advanced capitalist western societies with their dissolving sense of community and tradition to the emerging Asian and African countries with their clash of the old traditional, stable patterns and the new corrosive demands of industrialization. The pluralism of theology today is also a function of theology's response to new intellectual challenges to Christian belief, particularly from the world of the physical, human and medical sciences.

Recent theology has begun to make a virtue of necessity and to seek a theological rationale for theological pluralism (Rahner, 1961–; Sykes, 1984; Avis, 1986). In ecumenical theology and practice, the fact that there is a plurality of churches, beliefs and forms of worship and government is taken as axiomatic and does not seem to trouble us – a measure of the sea-change that has occurred in theology in the twentieth century. The fact that there are thousands of Christian denominations does not sit easily with intolerant and absolutist claims for one's own position (though the sense of perspective and perhaps humility thereby induced should not be equated with the extreme dogmatic relativism which has abandoned the quest for attainable truth).

Ecclesiology assumes greater urgency in times of conflict or renewal in the Church as old beliefs and structures are placed under strain. The Reformation, the Enlightenment and the French Revolution put Roman Catholic ecclesiology on the defensive until the Second Vatican Council. Protestant ecclesiology was reinvigorated through the influence of the religious revivals of the eighteenth century and thence through the work of Schleiermacher in Germany. German Protestant theology stimulated Coleridge, Thomas Arnold and Maurice to search for a renewed ecclesiology for an increasingly pluralist situation in England. By the same token High Church Anglican ecclesiology was revitalized by Newman, Palmer and Gladstone, among other leaders of the Oxford Movement. The ecumenical movement of the twentieth century received its impulse from the missionary expansion of the western churches (and thus ultimately from the eighteenth- and nineteenth-century religious revivals). But this original missionary motive, while by no means lost in the ecumenical movement, became transposed into a renewal of ecclesiology in the Faith and Order movement which became a component of the World Council of Churches at its formation in 1948.

Through bilateral and multilateral theological dialogues, all traditions of the Church have been compelled to reassess their self-understanding and their evaluation of other churches. The ecumenical encounter has generated a quest for Anglican ecclesial identity within the Anglican Communion. Some Protestant churches have begun to look again at the value of the historic episcopate in helping to realize the visible unity of the Church. Even the Eastern Orthodox, long-standing participants in the ecumenical process, are conducting something of an internal debate on the validity of their traditionally exclusive ecclesiology. But the most remarkable renewal of ecclesiology has taken place in the Roman Catholic Church, culminating in the constitutions on the Church and on ecumenism of Vatican II. Intense theological ferment on the subject of the Church, its authority, its ministry and its ecumenical identity has continued in the Roman Catholic Church since Vatican II. But during the pontificate of John Paul II the exercise of a strong central teaching authority (*magisterium*) has prevented this creativity from developing into a fully ecumenical policy.

In conclusion: ecclesiology is the department of Christian theology that takes the Church's self-understanding as its object. It is pursued in biblical, historical, systematic and practical modes. It draws on the resources of tradition and engages with contemporary culture. Ecclesiology may be defined, therefore, as *the critical study of the dominant models of the Church's self-understanding*.

A basic ecclesiology is in fact an essential item for every thinking lay Christian to carry in their backpack, for we cannot be Christians at all without the Church, 'the blessed company of all faithful people'. Therefore we need to be able to say what the Church of Christ is and how that particular branch of it to which we belong is related to the whole. Even more obviously, no ordained Christian minister can function without an ecclesiology. As clergy or ministers we receive our authority for ministry from Christ through the Church. Therefore we need to know what are the theological credentials – the defining ecclesiological characteristics – of the Church that has bestowed on us the authority to minister word, sacrament and pastoral care in the name of Christ.

2

The Quest for Anglican Ecclesiology

Anglicans tend not to debate passionately the nature and mission of the Church of Jesus Christ. Where two or three Anglicans are gathered together the most likely topic of conversation is the politics of the flower rota or the arrangements for the parish fête! However, there are signs that Anglicans are beginning to take ecclesiology more seriously than has been the case for many years. It is entirely appropriate that there should be an Anglican ecclesiology. For within the overarching definition of ecclesiology, as the study of the Church of Christ as such, the Church spoken of in the creeds, there are narrower, domestic applications of ecclesiology where the distinctive characteristics of a particular Christian tradition are explored, expounded and criticized. Within this plurality of ecclesiologies, there must inevitably be a place for an Anglican ecclesiology.

Supposing, for the sake of argument, that Anglicans were to borrow all their other doctrines from elsewhere, they could not exist, in the nature of the case, without an ecclesiology of their own. Since the churches of the Anglican Communion, with their ministries and sacraments, are not recognized as having full ecclesial reality by the two most ancient of Christian churches, the Roman Catholic and the Eastern Orthodox, how would Anglicans know that they belonged to the Christian Church without an ecclesiology that substantiated that claim? (On the aspect of this quesion concerned with Anglican ordinations ('orders'), see Avis, 1999). As Bishop Stephen Sykes has frequently insisted, 'It cannot be the case that there is no Anglican ecclesiology' (Sykes, 1994, p. 32).

It has been well said that 'Anglicanism, since its beginnings, has been forged on the anvil of ecclesiological controversy' (Philip Thomas in Sykes, Booty and Knight (eds), 1998, p. 250). It is the doctrine of the Church (ecclesiology) rather than the doctrine of salvation (soteriology) that has been the driving force of historic Anglicanism. Of course the two are bound up together and there cannot be one without the other. This is reflected in the ancient doctrine 'No salvation outside the Church' (*extra ecclesiam nulla salus*). What is meant by salvation and what is meant by Church in this dictum require considerable nuancing, but clearly they go hand in hand. Although salvation and the Church are two sides of the same coin, there may be a difference of emphasis in particular Christian traditions.

In the case of Anglicanism, its distinctiveness has been worked out in relation to ecclesiology rather than soteriology. When we think of Anglicanism, most of us do not immediately think of the salvation of our souls! The picture that probably comes into our minds is not John Bunyan's Pilgrim, with his back to the City of Destruction, toiling up a steep and rugged pathway with an enormous burden of sins on his back. It is more likely to be a homely picture of a parish church with its kindly but somewhat harassed vicar. It is, however, worth emphasizing in passing that Anglicanism, like all the many and varied forms of Christianity, is inescapably a way of salvation. Its liturgy, in the tradition of the Book of Common Prayer, is profoundly and seriously soteriological. Anglican worship arises from a heartfelt sense of human need and a thankful acceptance of the remedy provided by the grace of God.

Anglicanism is one of the humanly, historically conditioned institutional forms taken by that gracious saving action of God, through the ministry of word, sacrament and pastoral care, and our human response to it in faith and discipleship. This fact suggests that the Church is actually inextricably involved in the Anglican way of salvation and that we are not far out, after all, if it is the church, rather than some individualistic image of salvation, that first springs to mind when Anglicanism is mentioned. Let no one imagine that I am writing this book about the Church because I think that salvation is not important. Nothing could be further from the truth!

Yet Anglicans have never fully agreed about what sort of church theirs is and should be. There has been no single dominant Anglican ecclesiology. In recent times, this fact seems to have made Anglicans a little cynical about ecclesiology altogether; it has become the poor relation among theological disciplines and has been seriously neglected in theological education (in England at least), especially in the training of ordinands. Yet there are actually few areas of theology that are more fundamental than the study of the Church.

It is, therefore, gratifying to note that during the past decade or two, the issue of Anglican ecclesial identity has been promoted to a place near the top of the Anglican agenda. We might take the publication of Stephen Sykes' stimulating work *The Integrity of Anglicanism* on the eve of the 1978 Lambeth Conference of all Anglican bishops as marking the beginning of the current preoccupation with Anglican identity. But the question of Anglican ecclesial identity is not a new one. We are certainly not the first generation to be exercised by it. Lambeth Conferences, particularly those of 1930 and 1948, have provided classic statements of Anglican self-definition. This is how the 1930 Lambeth Conference defined the Anglican Communion:

The Anglican Communion is a fellowship, within the one, holy, catholic and apostolic Church, of those duly constituted dioceses, provinces, or regional Churches in communion with the see of Canterbury, which have the following characteristics in common:

● *they uphold and propagate the catholic and apostolic faith and order as they are generally set forth in the Book of Common Prayer as authorised in their several churches;*

> ⊚ *they are particular or national Churches, and as such, promote within each of their territories a national expression of Christian faith, life and worship; and*
> ⊚ *they are bound together not by a central legislative and executive authority but by mutual loyalty sustained by the common counsel of the bishops in conference. (Coleman, 1992, pp. 83ff; for analysis and commentary, see Avis, 1996.)*

In fact, however, the concern for Anglican identity can be traced back well beyond the Lambeth Conferences, which began in the second half of the nineteenth century (1867). The problem is perennial. It is as old as Anglicanism itself, but it has surfaced particularly strongly at times of greatest stress and conflict.

In the mid-sixteenth century, John Jewel (the first apologist for the reformed English Church) and Matthew Parker (Elizabeth's first Archbishop of Canterbury) attempted to define Anglican identity over against the rival claims of the Roman Catholic Church. At the end of the century, Richard Hooker devoted his treatise *Of the Laws of Ecclesiastical Polity* to defining and defending the integrity of the Anglican system or polity over against the radical Puritans who regarded the Church of England as still a fundamentally unreformed church because it did not conform in all respects to the pattern of 'the best reformed churches' – namely Calvin's Geneva – by expelling the residues of medieval Catholicism in liturgy, polity and doctrine. In the aftermath of the Civil War and during the Commonwealth, Anglicans in exile (like Cosin), or keeping a low profile in retirement (like Hammond), devoted their efforts to reconstructing the identity of the Church of England and were given the opportunity to implement, at least partially, the blueprint that they had devised at the Restoration of the monarchy and the Church in 1660–62. In the 1830s, Keble, Newman and others leapt to the defence of a conservative (both theologically and politically conservative) interpretation of Anglican identity in the face of the emerging pluralistic and incipiently secular state.

The issues that called forth the passionate dedication and unrivalled learning of earlier Anglican divines have not yet been laid to rest. They are still very much with us. The Roman Catholic Church still claims for the papacy an immediate, ordinary, universal jurisdiction over all local churches (dioceses), infallibility for its dogmas and unquestioning obedience to its day-to-day teaching on faith and morals (the ordinary magisterium). The Anglican polity with its sacramental principle and its historic episcopate still requires justification against the radical Protestant critique of all traditional structures. The status of the Church of England as a national church, by law established, on which all citizens have a claim and which is deeply implicated in the life of the English people, is still controversial, even though the terms of establishment have been continually modified and the pastoral situation is more strongly pluralistic than ever. The question of Anglican identity is still posed by all these factors; but there are two important new factors to be taken into account: the ecumenical movement and developments within the Anglican Communion. Let us glance at each of these.

As we have already noted, when churches take part in ecumenical dialogue that aims to clarify the differences of the past, remove unnecessary barriers to communion, and seek a basis for further steps to unity, it becomes all the more vital for them to have a clear sense of their historical identity. They need an awareness of the various factors that have shaped them as particular Christian traditions – Roman Catholic, Orthodox, Anglican, Lutheran, Reformed, Methodist, Baptist, etc. – and of the theological principles on which they have, historically, taken their stand. There can be little doubt that the work of the Anglican–Roman Catholic International Commission (ARCIC) and other bilateral conversations have concentrated the minds of Anglicans to reflect on their ecclesial identity. In this respect, Roman Catholic representatives have an advantage: there is clearly an enormous difference between a communion, such as the Roman Catholic Church is, with a central teaching office (or magisterium) and a clearly defined body of doctrine stated in authoritative documents, and a communion like the Anglican Communion which travels with fairly light doctrinal baggage, makes a virtue of dispersed authority and gives a constitutional role to laity and clergy in structures of representative church government.

The second factor that has heightened the question of Anglican identity today is the nature and future of the Anglican Communion, the worldwide family of legally autonomous but spiritually and pastorally interdependent churches that are in communion with the Archbishop of Canterbury. The growing strength and confidence of provinces in the developing world has intensified the centrifugal forces within the Communion. At the 1998 Lambeth Conference the battle-lines were drawn up between first and second world liberals and third world conservatives over human sexuality. The different speeds at which provinces are ordaining women to the diaconate, the priesthood and the episcopate has increased the stresses. Acceptance of the notion of 'impaired communion' between provinces that do not any longer enjoy a full mutual recognition of ministries, because of this issue, calls into question the reality of a coherent and unified Anglican identity. The possibility then arises of a diversity of interpretations of Anglican identity emerging within the Anglican Communion. The quest for fundamental axioms of Anglican ecclesial identity, that may prove stronger than individual theological stances or differences over policy, thus acquires an added urgency.

The Preface to the Declaration of Assent in the Church of England, which is used whenever a person is ordained or admitted to a new ministry, is a superb statement of the Anglican understanding of the Church on the part of one of the member churches of the Anglican Communion.

The Church of England is part of the one, holy, catholic and apostolic Church worshipping the one true God, Father, Son and Holy Spirit. It professes the faith uniquely revealed in the Holy Scriptures and set forth in the catholic creeds, which faith the Church is called upon to proclaim afresh in each generation. Led by the Holy Spirit, it has borne witness to Christian truth in its historic formularies, the Thirty-nine Articles of Religion, the Book of Common Prayer, and the Ordering of Bishops, Priests and Deacons. (Canon C15; ASB, p. 387; for analysis and commentary, see Avis, 1996)

3

Three Models of Anglican Self-Understanding

Anglicans have not always understood their church in the same way and there is far from being unanimity today between the three main traditions of churchmanship within Anglicanism: the evangelical or reformed; the Anglican catholic or traditionalist; and the liberal, broad church, central or non-party tradition. (The difficulty in finding the right word to describe these groups suggests that each contains considerable diversity. Though Anglican charismatics are most likely to be found among evangelicals, the charismatic movement has touched all parts of the Anglican family, bringing greater spontaneity in worship, renewal in spirituality and confidence in the power of the Holy Spirit.)

When we look at the Anglican understanding of the Church in historical perspective, we can discern three dominant models or paradigms of Anglican identity or self-definition – two explicit and one implicit. Let us consider them in turn.

THE NATION-AS-CHURCH MODEL

The nation-as-church model of Anglicanism held sway from the Reformation to the Oxford Movement. I have called this elsewhere the 'Erastian paradigm' (Avis, 1989a) – Erastianism being the theory of ecclesiastical government that gives the state a role in spiritual oversight, especially in applying sanctions, including excommunication. If we want a slogan for this model, it might be 'the citizen as Anglican'. Church and people, Christian and citizen, are regarded as one entity in a Christian commonwealth. Church and nation are coterminous. To be English was to be Anglican. All those born into the English nation were baptized into the English Church. You did not opt in; in the sixteenth century at least, you could not opt out. The nation-as-church model was the presupposition of the Anglican Reformers, Richard Hooker and the seventeenth-century Caroline divines. It was still fundamental to the ecclesiology of the Tractarians two hundred years later, though they gave it a different twist, as we shall see, and was equally important to the 'Broad Church' theologians: Samuel Taylor Coleridge, Thomas Arnold and Frederick Denison Maurice.

These Anglican theologians did not, of course, deny that there was only one Church and that it was a visible Church. But for practical purposes they thought of it as constituted by 'particular' or national churches. Only by emphasizing the integrity of particular churches over against the claim of Rome to immediate universal jurisdiction could they have succeeded in defending the Reformation of the Church. The nation-as-church model of Anglican identity was enforced by successive acts of uniformity and by legal penalties against dissenters – Roman Catholic or Protestant. The legal framework was progressively relaxed in the eighteenth century and was repealed on the eve of the Oxford Movement (the late 1820s and early 1830s), so actually precipitating a crisis of Anglican identity.

The sovereign was 'Supreme Governor' of the national church, not to perform sacraments or (less certainly) to define doctrine, but to have the ultimate oversight of all subjects in the spiritual as well as the temporal spheres. Though a lay person, the sovereign was anointed at his or her coronation, thus becoming a sacred figure, a symbol of the identity of the national church, pledged by the coronation oath to watch over and defend the privileges of the church.

At the accession of Charles I William Laud preached at the Chapel Royal, Whitehall. 'The King', he declared 'is God's immediate lieutenant upon earth, and the power which resides in the King is not any assuming to himself, nor any gift from the people, but God's' (Carlton, 1987, p. 53). Church and state, according to the injunctions issued by authority of Charles I in 1626, but drafted by Laud, 'are so nearly united together that they may seem to be two bodies, yet in some relations they may be accounted but as one in as much as they are both made up of the same men which are differentiated only in relation to spiritual and civil ends' (Carlton, 1987, p. 63).

As the throne began to totter, the rhetoric of divine right, undergirding the unity of Church and state, became the more shrill. In 1640 Convocation declared:

> *The most high and sacred order of kings is of divine right being the ordinance of God himself, founded in the prime laws of nature, and clearly established by express texts both of the Old and New Testaments. A supreme power is given to this most excellent order by God himself in the Scripture, which is that kings should rule and command in their several dominions all persons of what rank or estate soever, whether ecclesiastical or civil.*

> (Figgis, 1922, pp. 142f)

Parliament, with bishops in the House of Lords, was regarded as the synod of the Church, with the Convocations of clergy in the provinces of Canterbury and York as a check, and Parliament was indeed given authority in doctrine and worship.

All this is obviously not quite how English Anglicans think of their church today – and it is a far cry from the Anglicanism of other provinces of the worldwide Communion. Can we attempt to trace some of the factors that led to the demise of the nation-as-church model of Anglican identity?

◉ Pluralistic and centrifugal forces in English society could not be contained by the legal framework. The Civil War took the lid off the ferment and gave presbyterians, independents, and even more radical spirits their opportunity. Nonconformity became a major force in English society by the early nineteenth century.

◉ Parliament ceased to have credibility as the lay synod of the Church of England as Protestant Nonconformists, Roman Catholics and even non-Christians were admitted during the course of the nineteenth century. The demand for the Church of England to have its own legislative structure became irresistible, culminating in the Enabling Act of 1919, the foundation of today's synodical government.

◉ A succession of monarchs from the seventeenth to the nineteenth centuries seemed to fail the church. As protectors of the church's privileges and defenders of the faith, they proved themselves broken reeds. Charles I alienated a large proportion of the population. Charles II was a crypto-Roman Catholic and James II overtly Roman. Both sought to undermine the Anglican monopoly by bringing forward toleration measures that, by aiding all dissenters, would assist Roman Catholics. When James II was compelled to vacate the throne, he was succeeded by a Calvinist Dutchman, William of Orange. George I was likewise no Anglican, but a Lutheran, from Hanover. William IV had given his royal assent to the Whig legislation in the late 1820s and early 1830s that deprived the Church of England of wealth, monopolies and privileges, culminating in the suppression of a number of scandalously superfluous Irish bishoprics and archbishoprics, which traditional High Churchmen like Keble took as the crowning insult.

In England some significant traces remain of the nation-as-church model. The law of the church is part of the law of the land. The sovereign is still the lay supreme governor of the church – though the monarchy has become constitutional in relation to the church just as it has in relation to Parliament. The Prime Minister still plays a role in the appointment of bishops and deans of cathedrals, regardless of his or her own Christian affiliation, or lack of it. Parliament still functions as a longstop on ecclesiastical legislation emanating from the General Synod. Some bishops still have seats in the House of Lords. Substantial civic recognition is given to the Anglican clergy and the law of the land imposes pastoral obligations on them. Common religion – the inchoate religious beliefs and values of the unchurched – provides the clergy with many opportunities of pastoral ministry. The parish structure can only be justified in terms of a national church in which every citizen has both rights and duties vis à vis the church. The inherited resources of the Church of England, its endowments, belong within the framework of a national, established church and would seem to entail an obligation for the church and its clergy to make their ministry of word, sacrament and pastoral care available to all. (I hope to publish a fuller discussion of the mission of a national church in the near future.)

These conditions do not pertain elsewhere in the Anglican Communion, but the national church model persists when Anglicans outside England see themselves as having a mission to the whole community and to the nation, as they generally do (for the Anglican Church of Australia: see Kaye, 1995).

THE EPISCOPAL SUCCESSION MODEL

The episcopal succession model, which elsewhere I have called the 'apostolic paradigm' (Avis, 1989a), emerged in the late seventeenth century at the Restoration of the monarchy and the liturgy and episcopate of the Church of England. It was at this juncture that an important shift in the centre of gravity of the Church of England took place. From being an episcopal church, in which bishops were regarded as an ancient and even apostolic form of church government and were, moreover, endorsed by the civil authority ('the magistrate'), the Church of England became, so to speak, a self-consciously 'episcopalian' church in which episcopacy was regarded as the only God-given, scripturally warranted ecclesiastical polity. After the Restoration, the threefold ministry in historical succession became part of the foundational ideology of Anglicanism. However, the ecumenical consequences of this model only became fully developed in the attempt of the more extreme members of the Oxford Movement to 'unprotestantize' the Church of England. The sacred symbol of this model is not the sovereign but the bishop. Its slogan is 'Bishops are essential' – essential, that is, to the very existence (the *esse*) of the Church.

The transition from the nation-as-church model to the episcopal succession model was a gradual one, suddenly accelerated at the time of the Oxford Movement. In the seventeenth century it was widely acknowledged that bishops and kings stood or fell together. As James I famously put it, 'No bishop, no king'. At the Civil War, his words were fulfilled when Archbishop Laud preceded King Charles to the scaffold. Bishops and kings were equally sacred figures clothed with divine office. The sovereign appointed and invested bishops, while bishops, for their part, crowned the sovereign, attended at court and held high positions of state. But, as we have seen, the kings one after another seemed to fail the church. The bishops were left to fight for its claims unsupported.

In the Oxford Movement, the figure of the bishop emerged as an alternative sacred symbol to that of the sovereign. The Tractarians looked to the episcopate to save the church from the depradations of the Whig Government. In the first of the *Tracts for the Times* (1833), Newman urged the bishops, 'Magnify your office!' He recalled them to the example of the early Fathers who had sealed their testimony with their blood. Newman wrote that he could not wish the bishops a more blessed termination of their earthly course than the spoliation of their goods and a glorious martyrdom. This was not what most prelates of the Church of England by law established, under King William IV, were hoping for!

In the fourth of the Tracts, Keble reinforced the message. Only episcopally ordained clergy, incorporated within the apostolic succession, had the means of saving grace, efficacious sacraments, to dispense. Therefore, it was only within the Church of England that salvation could be assured to English people, vast numbers of whom were by now Nonconformist. This insistence became the keynote of the catholic revival in Anglicanism. The identity of Anglicanism was to be found in its episcopal orders within the historical succession. Now, while this gave a vital bond – at least in theory – with other episcopal traditions (i.e., Roman Catholic and Eastern Orthodox), it effectively cut Anglicanism off from Protestant bodies (which they did not recognize as having all the attributes of Christian churches).

To what extent is the fully fledged episcopal succession model a live option for Anglicans today? The fact is that it began to fail as soon as thought of. Newman confessed that it was merely a paper theory. He and his colleagues in the radical wing of the Oxford Movement actually contributed to its demise. The clergy of the catholic revival exalted bishops in theory, but proved thorns in their flesh in practice. The bishops themselves were reluctant to conform to the role that the Tractarians assigned them. When the then Bishop of Oxford (Bagot) distanced himself from the teaching of the Tracts, Newman was dismayed and his search for an alternative can be traced to that experience of rejection. When Tract 90 (in which Newman had attempted to reconcile the Thirty-nine Articles with the decrees of the Counter-Reformation Council of Trent) was condemned in 1841, the consequences for Newman personally were catastrophic: his alienation from the church of his baptism was complete (see Gilley, 1990). In the ritualist movement that emerged from the later Tractarian tradition, the notion of canonical obedience to one's bishop became highly precarious. The episcopal succession model failed in practice, but it failed in theory too. Its theological inadequacy can be summarized under several points.

◉ First, it could not deliver all the essential credal notes of the Church. It seemed to guarantee apostolicity (the continuity of the Church with the apostles) but not catholicity (the communion of local churches with the universal Church today). Through the historic succession, a church could feel itself in communion with the Church of the Apostles and early Fathers. But that in itself did nothing to bring that church into communion with the rest of episcopal Christianity. In Newman's case, this meant the Church of Rome, for Newman spared little thought for the significance of the Orthodox churches. So Newman was led to postulate what we might call an alternative apostolic succession – not merely one of the tactile transmission of holy orders, but one of continuity of ethos, of spirit, with the Christians of the early Church: simple, ignorant, superstitious, persecuted and poor as they were (that was their glory in Newman's eyes). Where would the early Fathers worship if they lived today? Newman asked himself. Not in a respectable Anglican parish church, nor in one of its grand cathedrals. Athanasius and Ambrose would be found kneeling before the sacrament in the Roman Catholic mission downtown. Newman's most passionate longing was to know himself to be united to those saints and scholars of the Church when it was still one and holy. And in this way he believed that he had achieved catholicity too (Newman, 1974).

- Second, the apostolic paradigm of Anglicanism was ecumenically sterile. It did little to facilitate steps to unity. Rome did not (and does not) recognize Anglican orders or eucharists (not even baptism then). Rome certainly did not (and does not) accept the episcopal model of Anglican identity. In the Roman Catholic system, the episcopate has no authority apart from its communion with and obedience to the pope (which Roman Catholic theology expresses in the term 'hierarchical communion'). Moreover, this paradigm naturally did nothing to encourage any movement towards the churches of the Reformation. If the episcopal succession was the *sine qua non* of the Church, non-episcopal bodies were not even in the picture. Such progress towards church unity as there has been in this ecumenical century, that has involved Anglicans (from the Church of South India scheme of 1947 to the Porvoo agreement between the British and Irish Anglican churches and the Nordic and Baltic Lutheran churches of 1996), has involved a compromise with this model of Anglican ecclesial identity in its absolute form.

- Furthermore, it made the historic episcopate essential to the very existence (of the *esse*) of the Church – something that the Anglican formularies specifically refrain from doing. The Lambeth Conference of 1930 stated: 'While we thus stand for the historic episcopate as a necessary element in any union in which the Anglican Church can take part ... we do not require of others acceptance of those reasons, or of any particular theory or interpretation of the episcopate as a condition of reunion.' The episcopal paradigm in effect excommunicated large portions of Christendom that lacked the historic succession and, in its strong form, denied them any assurance of salvation as they lacked the divinely appointed means. By seeking empirical guarantees of the credal apostolicity of the Church, it undoubtedly quenched the Spirit in unity matters.

◎ Ecumenical theology today has a broader understanding of the apostolicity of the Church. It sees it as carried not only by the episcopate, not even only by the ordained ministry, but by faithful continuance in the permanent attributes of the Church of the Apostles across a range of tasks that together comprise the mission of the Church. Ecumenical theology would hesitate to speak of the apostolic ministry until it has affirmed the apostolic community within which that ministry is placed and which it both serves and represents.

THE COMMUNION-THROUGH-BAPTISM MODEL

If the national church model and the episcopal succession model are both explicit in the history of Anglicanism, the third model, though firmly embedded in Anglican teaching and theological reflection, has never been explicitly articulated. It remains implicit and needs to be drawn out. The communion-through-baptism model is identical with what I have elsewhere called 'the baptismal paradigm'. If the national church model takes the anointed sovereign as its sacred symbol, and the episcopal succession model focuses on the bishop in tactile continuity with the Apostles, the communion model's sacred symbol is the foundation sacrament of Christian initiation, holy baptism. Putting it in slogan terms, we could say 'Baptism is the basis!' We might also care to note a progressive broadening out or egalitarianization (that is surely significant) in the succession of models of Anglican identity: from one sovereign to several bishops to many baptized believers. The baptismal model is non-hierarchical, corporate and communal.

The communion-through-baptism model aims to probe deeply into the living reality of the Church. It begins by asking, 'What makes the Church the Church?' It attempts to bring to light, and to subject to theological reflection, the inner spiritual vitality of the Christian community. It takes its starting-point from the true basics of the gospel: the baptism of Jesus as the inauguration of his mission and as endowing him with his unique messianic identity; and corresponding to that, the initiation of his disciples, then and now, into his Body through his Spirit in the sacrament of repentance, faith and union with Christ. The communion model takes as its key text 1 Corinthians 12.13: 'By one Spirit we were all baptized into one Body.' This approach brings out the immense ecclesiological significance of baptism as the instrument of our incorporation into Christ's messianic office as our Prophet, Priest and King – an incorporation which qualifies us to carry out prophetic, priestly and royal functions in the Church.

The communion-through-baptism model is richly represented in the official Anglican formularies and the Anglican theological tradition, from the Thirty-nine Articles to the Lambeth Conferences and from Richard Hooker to Frederick Denison Maurice. Some classical Anglican divines typically insisted that the fundamentals of the faith, which were required for salvation and professed in baptism, were the only proper basis of ecclesial communion. Stillingfleet, for example, claimed that the unity of the Church could only be attained when she made the foundation of her being the ground of her communion. Maurice reaffirms this principle when he insists that 'the language that makes Christ known to us is the only language which can fitly make the Church known to us' (Maurice, 1958, vol. 2, p. 125). The Lambeth Conferences have consistently proclaimed that it is baptism, with its accompanying baptismal faith, that makes us Christians and members of the Church. (I would refer to Avis, 1990, pp. 31–5, for further documentation that it would not be appropriate to reproduce here.)

But, someone may say, this interpretation of Anglican identity makes Anglicans no different from other baptized Christians. Precisely! Our fundamental Christian identity must be one that we share with our fellow baptized Christians throughout the world and the history of the Church. It would indeed be retrograde if, as Anglicans becoming more conscious of our historical distinctiveness and of the resources of our heritage, we were to attempt to define ourselves in a way that distanced us from Christians of other communions. It is solely on the basis of our solidarity with all Christ's people in his universal Body that we can then be free to pursue our distinctive Anglican way. Our fundamental identity is that given in Christ; confessional identities are secondary and require continual conversion to Christ and the gospel (for a searching discussion of this, see Groupe des Dombes, 1993).

That does not mean that there is nothing that is distinctive of Anglicanism. There are actually a number of features that contribute to Anglican identity within the family of Christian traditions (see Avis, 1998a). A central feature is its approach to questions of authority. There is the threefold appeal to scripture, reason and tradition (to give them in Hooker's order of precedence), but without a strong central magisterium to adjudicate on pressing issues when these three do not all point in one direction. There is the combination of episcopal pastoral leadership and oversight with conciliar, synodical church government in which laity and clergy are not merely consulted but have constitutional roles. There is the concentration on essentials, on central abiding truths, on fundamentals, that co-exists with much latitude in their interpretation. There is the tolerance and comprehensiveness of a range of internal traditions – catholic, evangelical and central – each touched by a spectrum of stances from conservative to radical. There is the weight that is placed on the corporate celebration of the liturgy and the lightness of touch with which juridical sanctions are invoked.

In addition to this constellation of features pertaining to authority in the Church, there are other elements of Anglican distinctiveness that should not be overlooked: A warm endorsement of the principle of inculturation of liturgy, theology and pastoral practice, as local customs, traditions and cultural expressions are used as a vehicle for the gospel as far as possible; the comprehending participation of the laity in worship, government and the discernment of doctrine; the tradition of vernacular liturgy and Bible reading; the combination of catholic order (the threefold ministry) with the Protestant affirmation of clerical marriage; the consequent role model of the clergy household within the community; and last but by no means least, the parochial approach to ministry which casts its mission in the mould of pastoral care, is not troubled by fuzzy edges, and seeks the integration of the committed Christian community with the wider local community through service.

CRITICAL CONSERVATION

Having affirmed the communion-through-baptism model of Anglican ecclesial identity, let us now ask whether there is anything of lasting value that deserves to be conserved from the nation-as-church model of Anglican identity, given that it must seem of merely academic interest to the greater part of the Anglican Communion. I suggest three items.

- The Church's mission is to all. Anglicanism can never be a sect. The Church of England is a territorial church and embraces all within its parishes who do not refuse its ministry. Its ethos is essentially inclusive, not exclusive. Most other churches of the Anglican Communion – even where they are not territorially based – would be guided by the same principle of inclusivity, being outward-looking and offering their pastoral ministry to all who are willing to receive it.

- The laity has a vital role in church government. The reformed English Church carried forward the central principles of the pre-Reformation conciliar movement: constitutionalism, representation and consent. In the historical nation-as-church model of Anglicanism, lay people were given rights that they did not enjoy in the unreformed medieval Church. They received the cup as well as the bread at Holy Communion; the Bible was available to them; services were in the vernacular. In Parliament, their representatives (though representation was very imperfectly conceived until the succession of reform acts in the nineteenth and early twentieth centuries) had a decisive voice in the doctrine and worship of the Church. The Reformation has been called the triumph of the laity. Today lay people are even more strongly represented in the councils of the Church – at parish, deanery, diocesan and national level. (In the Roman Catholic Church, while lay people are allowed to assist in worship, they have no place in the government of the Church.)

⊚ A branch of the Church has the authority to reform itself. This principle, that undergirded and legitimated the Reformation, remains crucial today. Anglican churches have, in recent decades, reformed their structures of government by establishing a synodical system, revised the rules for the conduct of the Church's life (canon law), rewritten their liturgies, and are now in the process of reforming their ministry by removing the barriers to the admission of women to the threefold order. Without giving blanket endorsement to all these changes, which need to be considered on their merits, we can see them as examples of particular churches attempting to reform and renew their life. It is salutary to recall that Rome denied that the Church of England had authority to reform itself in the sixteenth century and denies its right to reform itself now.

Is there anything of value that deserves to be conserved from the second model of Anglican identity, the episcopal succession paradigm? We recall that such proponents of this model as Newman and Manning gave it up to despair, that it has never received explicit endorsement in any Anglican formularies, and that – ironically – it is not countenanced by the Roman Catholic Church. Nevertheless, there is much that ought to be rescued from it which belongs to a sound ecclesiology.

- The bishop is the effective symbol of unity. There is an emerging ecumenical consensus that any united Church of the future will have bishops in the historical succession and that they will be regarded as symbols of unity. I have used the phrase 'effective symbols': bishops must above all relate to the communion (*koinonia*) experienced by a church through the sacraments – the mutual unconditional acceptance, founded on our common baptism into the Body of Christ, our common adherence to the baptismal faith, and the fulfilment and strengthening of this in the holy eucharist, the sacrament of unity. Though not of divine right, episcopacy can be justified, not merely as an ancient institution, but because the communion which is the life of the Church, and which transcends locality and particularity, requires it as its symbolic focus. Bishops are pre-eminently 'persons in relation'. However, if bishops put their unity function above all others – above teaching the faith, above defending truth, above efficient oversight and effective discipline, above leadership pointing to the future – then even unity itself will elude them.

- Bishops are entitled to canonical obedience from clergy and lay office-holders 'in all things lawful and honest'. We have already taken note of the common observation of historians that the catholic revival in the Church of England, that purported to exalt bishops, in practice undermined the authority of the ordinary. On grounds of conscience, Anglo-Catholic clergy often refused canonical obedience, particularly over ceremonial matters. This is linked with the next point.

- We should remain in communion with our bishop. It goes without saying that we should do all in our power to remain in communion with all those of our fellow Christians who are willing to be in communion with us. It is an extremely grave matter, spiritually, to break communion, exept over the most serious doctrinal or moral issue – one that must touch the integrity of the gospel itself and undermine our very salvation. If the bishop is the effective symbol of unity and communion, we have a special obligation to remain in communion with them. We do not have to agree with everything that our bishop says or does, but we are under an obligation to remain in communion. Breaking communion is not, in my view, an appropriate vehicle for expressing our hurt and dismay. It smacks of using the holy eucharist for political protest. Theologically, severance of communion can only be justified when the issue concerns the basis of our communion in God's act of salvation in Jesus Christ, our baptismal incorporation into the Body of Christ and the trinitarian baptismal faith itself (see Avis, 1990, ch. 5).

4

The Spirit of Anglican Ecclesiology

Christian churches have sometimes spoken of themselves as though they alone were the Church of Jesus Christ. They have tended to articulate the ecclesiology of their Church as though it were the only possible true ecclesiology – that is, without creating the necessary space in the mind between what can be said of any particular tradition and what may be said of the Church of Christ. This was inevitable where a church's ecclesiology included the claim that it was to be identified without remainder with the Church of Christ and that other ecclesial bodies were somehow outside the catholic Church. That claim has been modified as far as the Roman Catholic Church is concerned as a result of the Second Vatican Council, though ambiguity remains, and now questions are being raised even in the Orthodox Churches, though they certainly have not formally abandoned their claim to be the one true Church. When such absolute and exclusive claims are made for any church, a truly ecumenical approach to ecclesiology is ruled out. Obviously, the true Church cannot allow the views that heretics and schismatics may have of the Church to influence how it understands itself!

A distinctive feature of Anglican ecclesiology, I suggest, is that it has not been carried on in the insularity due to absolute and exclusive claims that has been typical of some other churches. I do not think Anglicans have ever made those claims. The Church of England, even at its most chauvinistic (say at the Restoration of the monarchy and episcopate in 1660–62) has never regarded itself as the only true Church; it has always recognized sister churches – Protestant, Roman Catholic or Orthodox. As a result, Anglican ecclesiology has openly drawn on the theological resources of other traditions; it has been practised in an ecumenical spirit and by a synthetic method. The early English Reformers, however harshly they may have spoken of Rome, recognized their affinity with the Reformation Churches on the Continent, regarding them as sister churches. The Thirty-nine Articles borrow unashamedly from the Lutheran Augsburg Confession (1530), especially in what they say about the Church. Richard Hooker (d. 1600) holds in his theological armoury not only the thought of St Thomas Aquinas, but the learning of the more recent and contemporary Roman Catholic divines, and deploys them with a good conscience at will. And when the differences between the Church of England and those Reformation churches widened from the late seventeenth century onwards, there grew up at the same time a less hostile attitude to the Roman Catholic Church among High Churchmen.

Hooker spoke of the various particular or national churches as being like the oceans of the world, separate but contiguous. Later writers employed the 'branch theory' of the Church to account for the existence of the Roman Catholic and Orthodox Churches alongside the Anglican. Anglican ecclesiology has never assumed that it is the only one there is and, therefore, has never made the mistake of exclusively identifying what may be said of Anglicanism with what may be said of the one, holy, catholic and apostolic Church of Jesus Christ. That seems to be an important clue to the distinctive spirit of Anglican ecclesiology. It is captured superbly in some well-known words of Michael Ramsey (later Archbishop of York and then of Canterbury) in *The Gospel and the Catholic Church* (1936) which I take as an aspiration for Anglicanism rather than a description of how it is:

For while the Anglican church is vindicated by its place in history, with a strikingly balanced witness to Gospel and Church and sound learning, its greater vindication lies in its pointing through its own history to something of which it is a fragment.

> Its credentials are its incompleteness, with the tension and the
> travail in its soul. It is clumsy and untidy, it baffles neatness and
> logic. For it is sent not to commend itself as 'the best type of
> Christianity', but by its very brokenness to point to the universal
> Church.

(Ramsey, 1936, p. 220)

However, that still leaves open the possibility that Anglicans
may have tended to assume that their ecclesiology was the best
available and had more to commend it than the alternatives. I
do not think that that assumption in itself is objectionable.
Individuals could hardly be expected to give heartfelt loyalty to
their particular Church unless they were convinced that it had
the edge over its rivals, ecclesiologically speaking. Whatever
contingent and imperfectly examined biographical and psycho-
logical factors contribute implicitly to one's commitment to a
Church, one must at least be satisfied as to its *raison d'être* – its
claims must be convincing. But it is when that theological
assurance begins to generate attitudes of complacency, super-
iority and arrogance that repentance and apology are called for.
So in suggesting that the spirit of Anglican ecclesiology is
marked by a ungrudging awareness of its incompleteness, the
absence of the sense of totality and finality, I mean that in an
objective sense. The spirit of individual Anglicans, in the
subjective sense, on the other hand, may frequently be
appalling!

5

The Threefold Appeal of Anglican Ecclesiology

In interpreting its own nature, Anglicanism has consistently made a threefold appeal. It has pointed to three sources that together constitute its ecclesial identity. Anglicans have appealed, first, to *the catholic tradition*, to historical continuity in the life, worship and ministry of the Church, and to the authority of the undivided Church of the early centuries; second, to *the principles of the Reformation*, grounded in a return to scripture and a recovery of the liberating gospel of free forgiveness for Christ's sake (justification by grace alone through faith) and the consequences of this for the reform of the Church in the light of the gospel – especially the right and duty of a particular branch of the Christian Church to reform itself in the light of scripture; and, third, to *the results of scholarly enquiry* ('sound learning'), applied to scripture and tradition, freely pursued and openly debated. Let us examine each of these a little more closely.

LOOKING TO THE CHURCH IN HISTORY – THE APPEAL TO CATHOLIC TRADITION

Anglicanism has never wavered in its conviction that it belongs to the catholic Church. This belonging has been put in various ways, the terms 'part', 'portion' or 'branch' being especially favoured. The catholicity of Anglicanism is essential to its self-understanding.

- The catholicity of Anglicanism has been justified *historically* by pointing to the antiquity of the British Church from which other provinces of the worldwide Anglican Communion have ultimately stemmed. The British Church had its representatives at a council of the catholic Church as early as 314 at Arles, and the Celtic Church flourished long before the arrival of Augustine of Canterbury in 597. Anglicans emphatically do not believe that their church originated at the Reformation.

- The catholicity of Anglicanism has been justified *theologically*, for Anglicanism incorporates and upholds the ancient structures of the catholic Church: the canon of scripture, the historic creeds, the dominical sacraments of holy baptism and the holy eucharist (set in the framework of liturgies that hark back to primitive forms), and the historic episcopate. The basis on which all these are accepted is the authority of the early undivided Church to interpret and clarify what remained unclear and incomplete in scripture itself as far as the life of the Church is concerned (and emphatically not as regards the way of salvation). These structures of catholicity are enshrined in the Chicago-Lambeth Quadrilateral that has been repeatedly affirmed since 1888 by Lambeth Conferences and the governing body of the Episcopal Church of the USA in particular.

- The catholicity of Anglicanism can be supported *polemically* by referring back to the abortive reforming councils of the pre-Reformation period. Anglican ecclesiology makes contact with conciliar rather than monarchical catholicism (see above). It accepts the authority of General Councils but denies that acceptance of the primacy and authority of the pope is essential to catholicity. The Anglican critique of certain features of Roman Catholicism has been informed, explicitly or tacitly, by the conciliar model of catholicism. Anglican polemicists have consistently pointed to Rome's inveterate tendency towards authoritarianism, with its attendant repression of theological liberty, its obscurantism, and its fixation on the juridical model of oversight in the Church. They have pointed out that the papal regime has proved historically incompatible with a fully conciliar view of catholicism – from the triumph of the fifteenth-century popes over the putative reforming councils to the imposition of conservative bishops against local wishes by the Vatican today. The synodical structure of the Anglican churches, on the other hand, with the vital role assigned to lay people, embodies this distinctive, conciliar understanding of catholicism.

It is, however, paradoxical that Anglicanism cannot now affirm its catholicity by identifying itself with any other extant tradition that also preserves intact the ancient structures of catholicism – particularly the historic episcopate. Anglican orders, eucharists and authority within its own borders are not recognized by the Roman Catholic Church. And for its own part, Anglicanism does not acknowledge the immediate universal jurisdiction of the pope, nor papal infallibility, nor the particular Marian dogmas that form the content of such infallible pronouncements as there have been. That does not mean that as Anglicans we can leave Rome out of the reckoning. The work of ARCIC (especially the *Final Report* of 1982 and *The Gift of Authority* of 1999) and the response by the House of Bishops of the Church of England to the papal encyclical *Ut Unum Sint* show a readiness to consider the principle of a reformed universal primacy (ARCIC, 1982; ARCIC, 1999; House of Bishops, 1997).

George Guiver CR has argued that Anglicanism is emasculated by its severance from the deep-rooted tradition of the Western Church:

Here is a cruse of wisdom and folly on the grandest of scales, and with a guts and readiness to acknowledge the dark physicality and bile of human nature, and the outrageous grandeur of our destiny, that cannot easily be found among polite Anglo-Saxons when left to themselves. Anglicanism's great merits bring with them the fault of an incapacity for the large-scale and audacious, and no great inclination to strive beyond homely horizons. Its gifts of comprehensiveness and

*understatement are never likely to set the world alight unless
they rediscover the deep mulch and vigour of the tradition of the
Western Church, whose whole history is part of our psyche, a
doorway to our very selves, if we would acknowledge it.*

(Guiver, 1990, p. 102)

Charles Gore, the great Anglo-Catholic bishop and theologian
(d. 1932), argued that what we seek in Anglicanism is not
Romanism without the pope, but catholicism without Rome
(Gore, 1884). Guiver does not believe that they are separable. It
would seem that a good deal more clarification is needed here
than ARCIC has been able to achieve so far.

The differences between Anglicans and Orthodox are
equally intractable, though they do not include disagreement
about jurisdiction or dogmas – thankfully, the Orthodox do not
think in terms of jurisdiction or dogmatic utterances. But
Anglicanism has not yet received the unequivocal approbation
of the Orthodox by their own criteria of 'unity of faith' and
'unity in the bishop' (see Avis, 1990).

Like Rome and the Orthodox (not to mention the Reformation Churches who would emphatically defend their own
catholicity), Anglicanism stands by its claim to belong to the
catholic Church, but it does this without unchurching other
claimants. However, since it cannot at present become identified with either of the two main catholic, episcopal, pre-
Reformation traditions, we are bound, I think, to conclude
that *the appeal to catholicism is necessary but not sufficient to define
Anglican ecclesial identity.*

LOOKING TO THE BIBLE – THE APPEAL TO
THE REFORMATION

Anglicanism is a reformed faith. Though the English Church
long predated the Reformation, it was decisively marked by the
events of the sixteenth century. They gave it its biblical centre
of gravity, its lay character, its earthing in family and home, its

intimate relationship with the English language. The very *raison d'être* of Anglicanism rests on an appeal to Reformation principles, for if Anglicans did not believe, with all the Reformers, that a branch of the ·Church has the inherent authority to reform itself, the events of the sixteenth century and the continued separate existence of the Anglican Communion could not be justified.

It has become customary for Anglicans to be rather apologetic about the Reformation. They cannot help feeling rather sheepish about the political manipulation, the dubious motives of Henry VIII, the wholesale dissolution of the monasteries, the compliance of Cranmer, the iconoclasm, the inadequate theology of the 1552 Prayer Book, followed by the astute compromises of the Elizabethan settlement. The apparent lack of principle is disturbing. Of course there is much to be ashamed of in what took place then. It must have seemed to many of the faithful that Christianity itself was being obliterated. But we need equally to remember that there is much to embarrass Christians of other traditions in their particular histories. It must be even more difficult for a devout Roman Catholic to come to terms with the corruption, ruthlessness and immorality of the pre-Reformation papacy because of the exalted claims that concurrently were being made for 'the vicar of Christ'.

The prevalent excessive uneasiness among Anglicans about the Reformation can be shown to derive from one particular strand of the Oxford Movement – the strand that diverged from the mainstream consensus of Anglican ecclesiology until then, namely, that the Church of England was a reformed church which took its stand on Reformation principles. These principles included crucially the paramount authority of scripture and the right and duty of a particular (that is to say, national) church to reform its life and worship in the light of scripture and the primitive Church, notwithstanding the veto of the Bishop of Rome. The irony of that departure from consensus is that it was founded on no great acquaintance with the thought and writings of the Reformers, but was instead profoundly influenced by unhistorical assumptions and crude comparisons between the sixteenth century and the nineteenth (see Avis, 1989a, part 3).

In essence, the more radical of the Tractarians – Hurrell Froude, John Henry Newman and to a lesser extent John Keble and Edward Bouverie Pusey – overlooked the aspiration of the Reformers to attain a true catholicity grounded in faithfulness to scripture and Christian antiquity. They discounted – if they ever knew – the disclaimers of the Reformers to be setting up a new Church, and their professed purpose to restore the face of the catholic Church so that it might once again reflect the purity and integrity of the Church of scripture and antiquity. Since, however, Rome also claimed the authority of scripture and antiquity, it is important to remind ourselves that the Reformers asserted the authority of scripture and antiquity over and above the contemporary empirical Church with its accumulated traditions.

Thanks to biblical and historical scholarship, we are far more conscious today than the Reformers were of the intimate interconnection between scripture and tradition, and are able to see scripture as set within the context of tradition, or as the authoritative element in tradition, as well as the paramount criterion for interpreting tradition. It becomes necessary then for us to transpose Reformation polemic into more contemporary terms and to talk about the authority of normative tradition over normed tradition, or of primary tradition over secondary tradition. But it is salutary to recognize that this way of looking at the matter was not entirely alien to the Reformers. It would appear to be implicit in their twofold appeal to scripture and the early Church ('antiquity'), for they believed them to be in harmony.

On this basis of scripture and primitive tradition, the Reformers rejected certain central aspects of medieval Christianity, particularly the claims of the papacy – claims to exercise universal jurisdiction, both spiritual and temporal; to enunciate doctrine without appeal; to possess the sole right to call a General Council and to preside over it; to give dispensations from the biblical injunctions (in the letter if not in the spirit). The Reformers also rejected any sacerdotal, mediatorial understanding of the ordained ministry, particularly as that was expressed in compulsory sacramental confession, the propitiatory sacrifice of the mass, and the quantitative conception of merit that could be accumulated and transferred. All these practices, they believed, could not be justified from scripture which contained all things necessary to salvation (Article 6 of the Thirty-nine Articles of Religion: see below).

On the same grounds, the Reformers embraced a number of positive reforms: that the Bible should be available in the vernacular; that the liturgy should also be in a language 'understanded of the people' and that they should participate in it; that the laity should receive communion in both kinds (the cup as well as the bread) and that communion should be more frequent; that the laity should have a role in the government of the Church and that the clergy should be free to marry. Underlying both negative and positive aspects of the Reformers' programme was the fundamental Reformation doctrine of justification through grace by faith and its corollary, the universal priesthood of the faithful. The logic of salvation full and free governed the specific practical reforms.

However, the English Reformers refrained from taking Protestant principles to their logical conclusion. For example, they did not claim that everything done in the Church must be justified by explicit reference to scripture. Neither Luther nor Calvin, and certainly not the English Reformers, insisted on a biblical blueprint for detailed patterns of worship or structures of ministry. They did not condemn bishops as such, and Luther and others even left the door open (or at least slightly ajar!) for a reformed papacy that would preach the gospel and correct abuses in the Church. The Reformers gave considerable discretion to the Church to take responsibility for its own life, government and worship. Luther regarded forms of ecclesiastical government pragmatically. Only the ministry of word and sacrament was absolutely essential. Oversight should be handled by the Christian magistrate (ruler) in whatever way seemed appropriate. Calvin did not assert the form of church government by elders (presbyterianism) as by divine right; that position arrived with his successor Beza. The English Reformers right up to Whitgift and Hooker, at the end of the sixteenth century, deliberately refrained from claiming divine right for episcopacy.

There was a consensus, though of varying degrees, that holy scripture had a God-given but restricted purpose: not to provide precept and precedent for the secondary questions concerned with the outward order of the Church, but to show the way of salvation. The Reformers made a space for 'things indifferent' (*adiaphora*). These were things that did not make a difference to one's salvation. In the case of Luther, Melanchthon and the English Reformers it was a very considerable space. In the case of Calvin and Zwingli, it was somewhat restricted. Richard Hooker was not comfortable about describing any aspect of the life of the Church as though it did not matter. Rather than 'things indifferent', Hooker preferred the phrase 'things accessory', i.e. accessory to the gospel. In other words, the Reformers looked not simply to the Bible but also to the Church and to human rational discernment. They took the Church of antiquity as a model of biblical interpretation and credited the contemporary Church with the Christian freedom to take responsibility for its affairs – provided always that the binding injunctions of scripture were not infringed and that man-made rules were not imposed on Christian consciences before the presence of God (*coram Deo*: Luther's catchphrase). We are bound then, I believe, to conclude that *the appeal to the Reformation is necessary but not sufficient to define Anglican ecclesial identity*.

LOOKING TO REASON – THE APPEAL TO SCHOLARLY ENQUIRY

Anglicanism sets out to offer a rational faith. It believes that its position in Christendom as a church that is both catholic and reformed can be justified by an appeal to sound learning. Its catholicism is not enslaved to tradition nor is its reformed character in bondage to biblical literalism. It is notably receptive to new insights deriving from 'secular' disciplines – receptive, not in the sense that it is prone to embrace these insights immediately, uncritically or without resistance, but in the sense that it gives scope and freedom to its clergy, as well as to its laity, to pursue such insights and to promote them without undue fear of ecclesiastical discipline or censure. In due course (though it never seems soon enough) it adapts its beliefs and practices to those insights (as we are seeing today with regard to the Christian feminist critique of sexism, androcentrism and patriarchalism in the tradition).

Such a vindication of Anglicanism's appeal to rationality could quote the celebrated dictum of Mandell Creighton (Bishop of London at the turn of the century) that the formula that best explains the position of the Anglican Church is that it rests on an appeal to sound learning. Neville Figgis CR (the Anglican political philosopher who died in 1919) – not by accident an admirer of Creighton – also could be called upon to second this opinion. However, several caveats should be entered immediately.

◉ All Christian churches have their own illustrious traditions of learning. Sound learning is not unique to Anglicanism, nor is Anglican sound learning necessarily more impressive than that of other traditions. I hardly need to illustrate the scholarship of the Roman Catholic Church. But as far as the Reformation Churches are concerned, the Protestant Reformers were humanist scholars steeped in the methods and conclusions of the Renaissance rediscovery of classical and Christian antiquity, and the Lutheran and Reformed Churches have enjoyed a theological distinction that is second to none. Although the scholarship of the seventeenth-century Anglican clergy was said to be the admiration of the world (*clerus Britannicus stupor mundi*), that distinction can hardly be claimed to have survived to the present day, generally speaking. The Anglican Communion is not paramount among Christian traditions for its scholarship and Anglicanism has been notoriously weak in the area of doctrinal or systematic theology.

- Anglicans cannot claim that the events of the sixteenth century and subsequent developments were a direct translation of the findings of scholarship into action. As Hensley Henson (Bishop of Durham before the Second World War) memorably said, it was not sound learning that filled the land with ruined monasteries and brought about bloodshed in abundance. However, Henson may have overstated his objection to Creighton's claim. The dissolution of the monasteries was not entirely unconnected with the findings of scholars that the religious vocation could not be supported from scripture and the very earliest period of the Church's history. And sixteenth-century polemicists never wearied of pointing out the contrast between the wealth and luxury of some religious foundations and the poverty and simplicity of the apostles. So while it is not necessary to claim a direct translation of sound learning into every aspect of church policy in order to assert a privileged place for scholarship in the Anglican scheme, it must be acknowledged that the record of the Church of England – to look no further – is not particularly illustrious in this respect: resistance to biblical criticism and to evolutionary theory being notable examples from the nineteenth century.

- It is not enough to show that Anglicans have often been extremely learned. A more pertinent question would be, What have they done with their learning? How have they deployed it? In answering that question, one would have to acknowledge that Anglican scholarship has frequently been employed polemically and tendentiously. It has been used to justify the unjustifiable, as when Hooker makes non-preaching clergy look like God's gift to the Church of England and non-residence in their benefice appear like a beneficial pastoral strategy (Hooker, 1845, *Ecclesiastical Polity*, V, lxxxi, 5–17). Learning has also been prostituted to make godly men caught up in the quandaries and compromises of their time look like cynical political timeservers – as in the radical Tractarian Hurrell Froude's reading of the Reformation.

◎ It is sometimes said that scholarship, with all its human failings, if allowed to be freely pursued, will correct its own shortcomings and excesses. The expression 'freely pursued' is the key to understanding the Anglican appeal to sound learning. It is not, as we have said, learning as such that is distinctive of Anglicanism, but the liberty that Anglicanism gives to scholars and theologians (even when they are priests or bishops) to research, to develop, to publish and to defend their ideas – and then to have them criticized and perhaps demolished by other scholars in turn. When Anglicanism appeals to sound learning, it assumes the freedom to pursue that learning. When it appeals to reason, it is the role of reason in rational discussion that it intends. And this openness and toleration applies not merely to the laity, as it would in some other traditions, but precisely to the clergy, the Church's 'official representatives', so to speak. Thus the distinctive Anglican comprehensiveness is entailed in the appeal to sound learning. Comprehensiveness in turn rests on the distinctive Anglican approach to authority and is an expression of it. Anglican authority is dispersed and corporate, though it presupposes a framework or foundation of central Christian beliefs and practices. Doctrinal and ethical decisions are not laid down by a central magisterium but are explored by the whole Church over a period of time until a consensus emerges and a position is reached that carries widespread conviction.

Thus the appeal to learning and reason in the context of mutual toleration itself depends on the framework provided by Anglican catholicity. It presupposes the hallowed structures of catholicism that Anglicanism has retained from the undivided Church (particularly the creeds, the liturgy and the oversight of bishops) which exert a restraining influence on unfettered speculation about the central Christian mysteries. Anglican clerical scholars, however radical they may appear in their explorations, are still required to celebrate the liturgy, say the creeds and give canonical obedience to their bishops. Although

Anglicanism's judicial constraints are weak, its moral and pastoral constraints are correspondingly strong.

Furthermore, the appeal to liberty of learning and to reason itself depends on the prior appeal to the Reformation with its principles of justification by faith which in turn gives rise to the doctrines of the universal priesthood and 'the freedom of a Christian man (woman)'. Christians are baptized into Christ's messianic Body and therefore participate in his prophetic, as well as his priestly and kingly, offices. They are thereby mandated to proclaim the mighty acts of God and to pursue the truth as it is in Jesus. Some 'liberty of prophesying' (in Bishop Jeremy Taylor's seventeenth-century phrase) is intrinsic to the Christian's baptismal status. When we see in this way that the appeal to sound learning and to rationality is itself dependent on the catholicity and the reformed character of Anglicanism, we are bound to conclude, I believe, that *the appeal to scholarly enquiry is necessary but not sufficient to define Anglican ecclesial identity*. Anglican ecclesiology makes not a single or double but a triple appeal. Catholicity, Reformation principles and scholarship freely pursued are mutually supportive and mutually interpretative.

TOWARDS AN ANGLICAN SYNTHESIS

Our analysis of the sources of Anglican identity has shown that, while appeal has been made consistently to the catholic tradition, to the principles of the Reformation and to sound learning and open debate, no one of these sources is sufficient by itself to define Anglican identity. However, taken together, in some kind of synthesis, they seem to offer a noble vision of a reasonable, reformed catholicism. But what sort of synthesis might this be? What kind of combination unites the catholic, reformed and scholarly components of the Anglican ideal? Several versions of the Anglican synthesis have been advanced (see further, Avis, 1986, ch. 7).

An historical accident?

This interpretation of the Anglican synthesis, as an accident of history, stresses the element of sheer historical contingency in Anglicanism, seeing it as merely a pragmatic adjustment to the changes and chances of the historical process. Hensley Henson claimed that the reformed English Church was the product of 'the cold sagacity of Tudor statecraft'. It cannot be denied that Elizabeth I's policy of comprehension was a balancing act intended to include all groups within the nation except those actually sworn to overthrow her regime (radical, 'separatist' Protestants and subversive Roman Catholics – by no means all). When she declined 'to make windows into men's hearts and minds', provided that they observed outward conformity, Elizabeth was not embracing any noble ideal of religious toleration, but exhibiting an astute sense of what strains the Church and nation could stand.

The element of contingency, of historical accident, is certainly present in the Anglican synthesis. But is there any Christian tradition that is without it? All communions of the Christian Church are, to a considerable degree, what they are now as a result of political factors, injected by emperors, kings, popes and prelates, and pragmatic adjustments to those factors – as well as being shaped by more diffuse economic and social movements. (That is not to deny that such bodies are, at the same time, the Body of Christ, brought into being by the grace of word and sacrament through the work of the Holy Spirit.) If Anglicanism is to any extent the outcome of historical accident, so are all the major Christian traditions. Nevertheless, the question remains: *Can a synthesis based purely on historical contingency have integrity?*

A cynical compromise?

If the first interpretation of the Anglican synthesis, the threefold appeal, stresses historical contingency, the second interpretation emphasizes the element of design. It claims that Anglicanism intentionally embraced a principle of calculated moderation. It sees the Anglican synthesis as a half-way house, a golden mean, a safe middle path through all extremes. Anglican apologetic in the seventeenth century celebrated the middle way (*via media*) between (as the poet-priest George Herbert put it) the allurements of Rome ('the painted harlot on the hill') and the uncomeliness of the Protestant churches ('the slovenly wench in the valley'); between (as Bishop Simon Patrick put it) 'the meretricious gaudiness of the Church of Rome and the squalid sluttery of fanatic conventicles'; between (as the politician George Savile put it) 'the lethargic ignorance of popish dreams' and the 'frenzy of fanatic visions'. The language of these earlier divines seems offensive in this polite ecumenical age and reveals how far we have come from the ecclesiastical trench warfare of the seventeenth century. The historian Thomas Babington Macaulay gave this interpretation his *imprimatur* when he pointed out the compromise involved in a church which had (as he saw it – not entirely accurately) Protestant Articles of Religion but a 'popish' liturgy; which retained bishops but without making them of the essence (*esse*) of the Church; which rejected transubstantiation but 'required her children to receive the memorials of divine love meekly kneeling upon their knees'; which, while abrogating compulsory sacramental confession, 'gently invited the dying penitent to confess his sins'. Archbishop William Temple, the great Anglican synthesizer of the twentieth century, saw Anglicanism as splitting the difference between bare Protestantism and (pre-Vatican II) Roman Catholicism.

It is not difficult to criticize this model. What becomes of the middle way, construed like this as the avoidance of extremes, when the 'extremes' move towards the middle – when, for example, the Roman Catholic Church reforms itself, as at the Second Vatican Council, throwing off such quantities of 'meretricious gaudiness' and 'lethargic ignorance' as might offend a rather Protestant Anglican conscience; or when Protestant churches themselves come to be perceived as standing more for sobriety and sincerity than for 'slovenliness' or 'fanaticism'? Macaulay was no theologian and his analysis is flawed. He underestimated the catholicity of the Thirty-nine Articles, especially the first ten, and overestimated the continuity between the Book of Common Prayer and its medieval liturgical precursors. William Temple rather discredited his own version of the *via media* by actually admitting that Anglicanism tended to 'sit on the fence'.

The model of the Anglican synthesis as a contrived compromise does certainly attempt to do justice to the characteristic moderation and balance of Anglican theological method – what John Henry Newman called its 'calmness and caution' and Paul Elmer More described as its 'love of balance, restraint, moderation, measure'. But these virtues are capable of a more suspicious interpretation. They are the very qualities that permit unreformed practices and the abuse of power and privilege to flourish. They hardly generate the spiritual dynamism that causes the gates of hell to quake! This approach points less to the theological discrimination that picks its way through the pitfalls of heresy and schism, and more to the fearful mediocrity that is motivated by timidity, complacency and indolence. Can this ever have integrity?

Binding together?

A true synthesis, one that has theological integrity, cannot be attained by trusting to the accidents of history or by resorting to cynical compromise. Only some kind of creative tension or dialectical interaction can generate genuine synthesis out of the threefold appeal that Anglicanism makes. In the mid-nineteenth century, F. D. Maurice rejected the compromise formula of Anglican ecclesial identity. The Reformation, Maurice insisted, was not a cowardly or cunning compromise between incompatible extremes. The catholic (traditional) and reformed (biblical) elements reacted upon each other, producing a 'healthy effervescence'. As yet, he claimed, no neutral salt had resulted from the combination! Maurice was seeking a critical and creative comprehension in which the positive truths to which each tradition witnessed (but which became distorted in isolated systems) would be acknowledged and given free rein (for substantiation and references for Maurice, see Avis, 1989a, ch. 16).

Maurice's insights were developed a century later by Michael Ramsey (later Archbishop of Canterbury), to whom I owe the phrase 'binding together'. In the Anglican vocation, according to Ramsey, the paramount authority of the gospel (the Reformation's contribution), the given reality of the Church catholic (which comes down to us through living tradition) and sound learning (or interaction with the modern world and its discoveries) are 'bound together'. It is when they are torn asunder and elaborated systematically in isolation that you have the distorted ideological systems: biblical literalism (fundamentalism); blinkered traditionalism infused with uncritical nostalgia; and arrogant rationalism that subjects the mystery of Christian revelation to its own narrow analytical criteria. But when bound together and held together in a community life of prayer, study and service, the three vital ingredients of the Anglican appeal interact – stimulating, criticizing and modifying each other in a real and living synthesis (Ramsey, 1936).

In conclusion, perhaps we can take our cue from the realm of psychotherapy. In the Jungian approach particularly, mental and spiritual wholeness comes from recognizing, accepting and reconciling the tensions that emerge from deep in the psyche, predominantly from the unconscious. So it is with 'the mind of the Church'. The first step is to acknowledge and confront the tensions – and that can only be done when there is toleration and spiritual liberty. The second step is to accept the fact of these tensions and to engage with them and in so doing to release life-giving energy for the Church's theological exploration and pastoral mission. As tensions are examined, misunderstandings can be resolved, stereotypes can be overcome, common ground can be discovered and some degree of genuine reconciliation can be attained.

This suggests the important truth that it is precisely *people* that must be bound together before ever principles can be. That binding together is given already in our common baptism. It is articulated and expressed at the Peace in the eucharist, using the words of scripture: 'We are the body of Christ. By one Spirit we were all baptised into one body. Endeavour to keep the unity of the Spirit in the bond of peace!' The binding together is realized and strengthened in the Communion. Thus baptism and the eucharist provide the primary ecclesiological condition for the mutual acceptance of one another as fellow Christians, united with one another through our union with Christ. It forms the basis for a synthesis that is not merely a meeting of minds, but a true communion (*koinonia*) in the Spirit.

6

The Sources of Anglican Ecclesiology

THE BIBLE

Anglicanism draws on a number of sources in working out its understanding of the Church. Primarily, of course, it acknowledges its dependence on holy scripture as containing all things necessary to be believed or performed in order to attain salvation (Article 6 of the Thirty-nine Articles). For most of Anglican history, the scriptural requirements for salvation would have been regarded as including baptism and probably holy communion. Moreover, even the creeds are held to derive their authority from scriptural warrant for their doctrine (Article 8).

The Bible is read extensively and comprehensively in Anglican services ('the lessons') and lay Anglicans have long been encouraged to study the Bible themselves. A fundamental principle of the Reformation was that the Bible should be available to all in their own language. Anglicanism shares the Reformation's implicit faith in scripture as able to instruct the ignorant, reform the wayward and convey clearly the way of salvation through Christ.

This way of understanding the authority of scripture entails that the Bible is not upheld as a source-book of binding rules and precedents for every aspect of the Church's life. The English Reformers regarded the outward ordering and government (polity) of the Church as of secondary importance and believed that a degree of freedom was given to the Church, under the magistrate (the civil ruler), to enact what seemed fitting, both in its worship and government. Richard Hooker reinforced this principle of freedom by grounding it in the divine reason by means of which God providentially orders the universe through natural law. But Hooker believed that to abandon episcopacy would be to depart from the apostolic pattern of the Church. This commitment to the ancient threefold ministry of the Church became, by the seventeenth century, a non-negotiable platform of Anglicanism. Thus, in Anglicanism scripture shows the way of salvation but reason and tradition play their part in shaping the life of the Church.

TRADITION

Tradition is a notoriously ambiguous term. It may have a narrower or broader meaning. Ecumenical theology has helped to clarify the range of meanings. In the narrow sense tradition (sometimes spelt with a capital T) stands for the central truths of Christianity, the faith once delivered to the saints, the gospel, the charter principles of the Church. In the broader sense tradition embraces the entire ongoing life of the Church in all its diversity, like a great stream carrying the life of the church down through the centuries. In Anglicanism, tradition is usually understood in the first sense, as early or normative tradition – the tradition of the catholic Church, going back beyond the Reformation to the legacy of the undivided and 'primitive' (i.e., original, uncorrupted) Church.

Anglicanism derives its insistence on the two dominical sacraments (i.e., the sacraments of baptism and the eucharist, instituted by the Lord) from scripture itself. But it draws its use of the creeds, the canon of scripture and the historic episcopate from the tradition of the early Church. Anglicanism obviously recognizes the validity of the tradition of the undivided Church in supplementing and interpreting what is revealed in scripture – not about the essential truths of faith or about the way of salvation, which are held to be clearly revealed in the Bible, but about the common life, belief and order of the Church. The catholicity of Anglicanism rests on a recognition that the Church is not only a mystical entity, known only to God, nor merely a local gathering of people for worship, but a visible society that is both divine and human, spanning the globe and persisting through history. The structures of the Church are not solely derivable from scripture (few, in any tradition, would claim that they were).

However, as we have already noted, the authority of tradition in Anglicanism is subordinated to that of scripture. Thus Canon A5 of the Church of England states that the doctrine of that Church 'is grounded in the Holy Scriptures, and in such teachings of the ancient Fathers and Councils of the Church as are agreeable to the said Scriptures'.

THE HISTORIC FORMULARIES

The Preface to the Declaration of Assent (Canon C15) of the Church of England states that the historic formularies bear witness to Christian truth. But what are the historic formularies? The Preface mentions the Thirty-nine Articles of Religion, the Book of Common Prayer and the Ordering of Bishops, Priests and Deacons. Let us look at these in turn before asking whether they need to be supplemented by other historic sources.

The Thirty-nine Articles

The Articles of Religion are derived from a series of doctrinal statements put out by the bishops and the king during the reign of Henry VIII. The Forty-two Articles appeared in 1553 and these were reduced to 39 ten years later. The Articles in their present form were issued in 1571 under Elizabeth I. A cursory glance at the Articles will show that they are not a complete account of Christian doctrine, even less an Anglican systematic theology. They are in fact a response to matters of controversy in the sixteenth century. They make certain central affirmations directed against several specific targets: anti-trinitarianism, Roman Catholicism and radical Protestantism.

- Speculative heterodoxy in the doctrine of God and in Christology is combatted in the first five Articles which affirm the trinitarian and Christological doctrines of the undivided Church. For example: 'There is but one living and true God ... And in unity of this Godhead there be three Persons, of one substance, power, and eternity; the Father, the Son, and the Holy Ghost' (from Article 1).
- Roman Catholicism, for whom Queen Elizabeth was a heretic, an outlaw and an impostor, is tackled in Articles 6, 11, 21, 22, 24, 30, 31, 2, 34, 7. For example: 'The Bishop of Rome hath no jurisdiction in this realm of England' (from Article 37).
- Radical Protestants, who rejected the union of Church and state and advocated gathered communities of more perfect Christians, are attacked in Articles 23, 26, 37, 38. For example: 'It is lawful for Christian men, at the commandment of the magistrate, to wear weapons, and serve in the wars' (from Article 37).
- Finally, a more extreme form of Calvinism than was acceptable in the Church of England is referred to in Article 17 on predestination and election. The approach here discourages speculation and encourages humble trust and practical obedience: '... we must receive God's promises in such wise, as they be generally set forth to us in Holy Scripture: and, in our doings, that Will of God is to be followed, which we have expressly declared unto us in the Word of God.'

The Book of Common Prayer

The Book of Common Prayer (BCP) in its classical form dates from 1662 when Anglican liturgical worship was reimposed by the Act of Uniformity following the Commonwealth under Oliver Cromwell. Earlier Prayer Books had been compiled by Thomas Cranmer in 1549 and 1552, the latter being the more Protestant of the two. The 1662 Book of Common Prayer was a compromise between the two positions. The teaching of the BCP (regarded as distinct from the Thirty-nine Articles and the Ordinal) is normative for the Church of England and many other churches of the Anglican Communion (though some have adapted the 1662 form). However, doctrine is taught only implicitly and tacitly in the liturgy. For example, generations of Anglicans have imbibed a particular understanding of the doctrine of the atonement from the Prayer of Consecration at the Holy Communion:

> *Almighty God, our heavenly Father, who of thy tender mercy didst give thine only begotten Son Jesus Christ to suffer death upon the Cross for our redemption; who made there (by his one oblation of himself once offered) a full, perfect, and sufficient sacrifice, oblation and satisfaction, for the sins of the whole world.*

It is significant that this passage portrays the death of Christ as a sacrifice; and it is equally significant that it does not use the term 'propitiation' (though this term is used in Article 31 and in the Comfortable Words). An interesting situation has developed with the widespread use of the Alternative Service Book 1980 (ASB), which does not have the same canonical authority as the BCP 1662 as a standard of doctrine in the Church of England. For example, the ASB does not use the expression 'satisfaction' of the death of Christ (for a comparison between the doctrines of the atonement that are found in the BCP and the ASB respectively, see the appendix to the Church of England's Doctrine Commission report *The Mystery of Salvation*, 1995).

On the relation between liturgy and doctrine, Louis Weil comments: 'It is not that the liturgy is a didactic tool, but rather that it inevitably articulates an underlying theology.' Weil continues:

> *The Book of Common Prayer is for Anglicans far more than a collection of rites. Within Anglicanism the Prayer Book is a living expression of the profound union between what we believe and what we pray; [it is] a doctrinal document, not because it may contain such didactic materials as a catechism, or historical materials of doctrinal significance, but because it is in corporate*

worship that Anglicans find the common ground for their profession of faith.

(Weil in Sykes, Booty and Knight (eds), 1998, p. 67)

The Ordinal

The authorized form for the ordination of bishops, priests and deacons is found (as far as the Church of England is concerned) in both the BCP and the ASB. There is a difference of emphasis between the two with the ASB weakening the BCP's claim that the threefold order goes back to the Apostles. However, both books insist on ordination by a bishop in the historical succession and this is common to all churches of the Anglican Communion. The Ordinal is the last of the formularies mentioned in the Preface to the Declaration of Assent.

The ASB Ordinal gives some fine definitions of the three orders of ordained ministry and these can be supplemented from the Canons.

- *Deacons* are in holy orders, unlike Readers or other lay ministers. They have a ministry of word and sacrament, assisting the parish priest liturgically and pastorally. They have a special care for all in need. The diaconate is usually regarded as a probationary year before priesting, but Anglicanism also recognizes a distinctive or permanent diaconate to which some may be called.
- *Presbyters* or priests have a ministry of word, sacrament and pastoral oversight (delegated by the bishop). Unlike deacons, presbyters have authority to preside at the eucharist, pronounce absolution to the penitent and give a blessing. They lead and preside at the eucharist because they lead and preside in the Christian community (see House of Bishops, 1997, *Eucharistic Presidency*).
- *Bishops* are the chief pastors in the local church or diocese (the expression 'local church' being rather a theological technical term for the sphere of the bishop's ministry) with oversight of clergy and laity and responsibility for implementing the canon law of the Church where pastoral discipline is

required. Bishops are the principal ministers of the sacraments and teachers and guardians of the faith, with the responsibility for providing for the ministry of word, sacrament and pastoral care throughout the diocese. Both individually and as a college, bishops lead the Church and share the government of the Church with laity and presbyters (sometimes deacons).

The canons

The first of the sources of Anglican ecclesiology that ought to be added to those referred to in that Preface is the canon law of the Church. The canons of a particular church normally contain certain important ecclesiological statements, and in this connection the canons have suffered undeserved neglect. However, Anglican churches are not 'confessional' churches possessing formal and definitive statements of their beliefs in the form of law. Anglican canon law normally points to doctrine stated elsewhere.

The present form of the canon law of the Church of England goes back to the beginning of the seventeenth century, though there was an abortive attempt by Cranmer to devise a reformed canon law in the previous century. The twentieth century has seen substantial revision of the canons, first by Archbishop Geoffrey Fisher and latterly by the General Synod which is constantly legislating. The presupposition of Anglican canon law is the catholicity of the Anglican churches as part of the catholic Church of Christ (Church of England Canon A1). (For an authoritative study on Church of England canon law in the context of the complete legal position, see Doe, 1996; for a comparative study of canon law in the churches of the Anglican Communion, see Doe, 1998; and for the history of the texts, see Bray, 1998.)

The Lambeth Quadrilateral

The Quadrilateral is one of the doctrinal standards of Anglicanism which needs to be added to those which have canonical authority. It clearly has a particular relevance to ecclesiology.

The Lambeth Conference of 1888 gave its endorsement to a modified version of four articles agreed at the General Convention of the Protestant Episcopal Church of the USA (now ECUSA) two years earlier in Chicago. These in turn were adapted from proposals put forward by William Reed Huntington in *The Church-Idea: An Essay Towards Unity* in 1870 which has justly been described by J. Robert Wright as 'probably the most significant American Anglican work on ecclesiology' (Wright, 1990, pp. 253f). In an American context it is, therefore, appropriate to refer to it as the Chicago-Lambeth Quadrilateral, but we should not forget that it was the Lambeth Conference that gave the Quadrilateral its authority for the Anglican Communion.

The four articles are intended to comprise the essentials that Anglicans would insist on in any reunion of the churches. The Quadrilateral has been frequently reaffirmed both by ECUSA and the Lambeth Conferences since then (most recently by the 1998 Lambeth Conference) and is a firmly established authority for Anglican ecclesiology. The four principles are:

- 'The Holy Scriptures of the Old and New Testaments, as "containing all things necessary to salvation", and as being the rule and ultimate standard of faith.'
- 'The Apostles' Creed, as the Baptismal Symbol; and the Nicene Creed, as the sufficient statement of the Christian Faith.'
- 'The two Sacraments ordained by Christ himself – Baptism and the Supper of the Lord – ministered with unfailing use of Christ's Words of Institution, and of the elements ordained by him.'
- 'The Historic Episcopate, locally adapted in the methods of its administration to the varying needs of the nations and peoples called of God into the Unity of his Church.'

Other notable statements of the Lambeth Conferences

The teachings of the Lambeth Conferences supplement the Quadrilateral. Outstanding among them is the 'Appeal to All

Christian People', issued by Lambeth 1920, which significantly described all those who had undergone trinitarian baptism as members of the Christian Church, and invited the churches to seek together for unity.

Another seminal statement of the Lambeth Conferences is that on the dispersed nature of Anglican authority issued by Lambeth 1948 and deservedly regarded as a classical definition of the nature of Anglicanism. It is worth quoting in full:

> *The positive nature of the authority which binds the Anglican Communion together is ... moral and spiritual, resting on the truth of the Gospel, and on a charity which is patient and willing to defer to the common mind.*
>
> *Authority, as inherited by the Anglican Communion from the undivided Church of the early centuries of the Christian era, is single in that it is derived from a single divine source, and reflects within itself the richness and historicity of the Divine Revelation, the authority of the eternal Father, the incarnate Son, and the life-giving Spirit. It is distributed among Scripture, Tradition, Creeds, the Ministry of the Word and Sacraments, the witness of saints, and the* consensus fidelium, *which is the continuing experience of the Holy Spirit through his faithful people in the Church.*
>
> *It is thus a dispersed rather than a centralised authority having many elements which combine, interact with, and check each other; these elements together contributing a process of mutual support, mutual checking, and redressing of errors or exaggerations in the many-sided fullness of the authority which Christ has committed to his Church. Where this authority of Christ is to be found mediated not in one mode but in several we recognise in this multiplicity God's loving provision against the temptations to tyranny and the dangers of unchecked power.*

The classical Anglican theologians

Anglicanism does not acknowledge any human teachers as definitive – unlike St Thomas Aquinas in Roman Catholicism,

John Calvin in the Reformed Churches or John Wesley in Methodism. However, the Anglican divines of the late sixteenth to the early eighteenth centuries – from Richard Hooker to Daniel Waterland – are generally recognized as possessing unrivalled wisdom and insight (though they remain men of their time and they do not, of course, completely agree with each other). Recently this tradition has suffered from disgraceful neglect in theological education and ordination training (especially in England), but that cannot alter the fact that their thought was formative of Anglicanism and that they belong to the common inheritance of the Anglican Communion. While they obviously need to be supplemented by more modern interpreters of Anglicanism, including those not from England, they hold an unsubstitutable place in the Anglican inheritance of faith.

Richard Hooker (1554–1600) is in a class of his own here as the prime architect of Anglican ecclesiology and the most effective defender of the Elizabethan settlement of religion which established the principle of comprehension or toleration that is intrinsic to Anglicanism. Both the style and content of Hooker's work, though not easy for the modern student to follow, operate at such an elevated level that they are a literary and theological education in themselves. (For an introduction to Hooker and many other classical Anglican divines, see Avis, 1989a; see also Percy, 1999. A classical anthology of Anglican writing of the seventeenth century is More and Cross (eds), 1935.)

7

The Shape of Anglican Ecclesiology

THE CHURCH

Anglicans understand the Church (this section follows the outline of the Church of England's draft statement to Churches Together in England as part of the Called to be One programme: see CTE, 1996) to be primarily the one, holy, catholic and apostolic Church, the Church of Christ. They believe that they belong to the Church of Christ. But they recognize that other, non-Anglican Christians, as individuals, also belong to the Church. They recognize that other Christian bodies corporately also belong to that Church. They affirm that each Anglican church within the Anglican Communion is itself truly the Church, but they do not claim to comprise the Church without remainder. Anglicans have used, therefore, the terms 'part', 'portion' or 'branch' to describe both their own church and other churches.

> The Episcopal Church of the USA defines itself accordingly as 'a constituent member of the Anglican Communion, a Fellowship within the One Holy Catholic and Apostolic Church, of those duly constituted Dioceses, Provinces, and Regional Churches in communion with the See of Canterbury, upholding and propagating the historic Faith and Order as set forth in the Book of Common Prayer'.

Anglicans maintain that the doctrine, worship, ministry, sacraments and government of their churches are those of the Church of Christ and that they are owned and blessed by the Holy Spirit. Anglican churches resolutely affirm their apostolicity and their standing as true churches of Christ. Their trust deeds (such as the canons) typically do not allow their members (in practice, their clergy) to deny this. Anglicans are deeply offended when the catholic and apostolic credentials of their church are impugned (for example by the Roman Catholic Church's condemnation of Anglican orders in 1898). They hold as strongly as Roman Catholics that the designation 'catholic' fully belongs to their church and in the creed they affirm that the Church is one, holy, catholic and apostolic.

Anglicans in England have consistently held that the Church of England is the ancient catholic Church in that land and they profoundly resented the imposition or restoration of the Roman Catholic hierarchy in 1850. They condemned it as a piece of territorial aggression and it aroused feelings of anger not unlike those generated by the Argentinian invasion of the Falkland Islands in 1982. That is not, of course, how the ecumenical movement regards the plurality of churches, and it is clearly unhelpful to contest the right of any of the numerous branches of the Christian Church to pursue their mission anywhere. But that greater ecumenical realism does not imply any dilution of the claim to catholicity of the Anglican churches. It merely entails that they do not for one moment deny that other churches are also catholic and apostolic.

At the same time that they resolutely uphold the ecclesial standing of their church, Anglicans readily acknowledge that, like all branches of the Christian Church, without exception, Anglicanism is provisional and incomplete in the light of the Church that is spoken of in the creeds as one, holy, catholic and apostolic. Anglicans believe that these credal attributes of the Church will only be fully revealed eschatologically, when God's saving purpose is revealed in the end time. This entails the important admission that the fragmentation of the Church into various parts or branches is not the definitive state of the

Church or what God wills for it. Here Anglicans are, in effect, saying: 'We are the Church. You also are the Church. But none of us is the Church as it should be.' This acknowledgement of the incompleteness of one's own church and recognition of the ecclesial reality of other churches generates the commitment to the quest for Christian unity. Anglicans have been in the forefront of leadership of the ecumenical movement. Here again we glimpse something of the distinctive ethos of Anglican ecclesiology.

Anglicans believe that the Church on earth is united with the Church in heaven in the communion of the saints (*sanctorum communio*). They speak of 'the Church Militant here in earth' and the Church triumphant in heaven. They worship God together with 'Angels and Archangels, and with all the company of heaven'. The service 'At the Burial of the Dead' in the Book of Common Prayer (1662) includes the prayer:

> *Almighty God, with whom do live the spirits of them that depart hence in the Lord, and with whom the souls of the faithful, after they are delivered from the burden of the flesh, are in joy and felicity: We ... beseech[ing] thee, that it may please thee, of thy gracious goodness, shortly to accomplish the number of thine elect, and to hasten thy kingdom; that we, with all those that are departed in the true faith of thy holy name, may have our perfect consummation and bliss, both in body and soul, in thy eternal and everlasting glory.*

Anglicans acknowledge that the Church of Christ on earth is manifested at various 'levels', from the universal to the very local.

◉ First, there is the *universal* Church which, though outwardly divided, consists of all Christians united to Christ in the Holy Spirit through faith and baptism and ordered in their various communities under the ministry of word, sacrament and pastoral oversight. Anglicans unequivocally recognize their fellowship with all the baptized, whatever their Christian tradition or denominational allegiance may be. The Book of Common Prayer (1662) speaks of Christians as 'very members incorporate in the mystical body of thy Son, which is the blessed company of all faithful people'.

⊛ Second, there are *provinces*, usually national churches, of which the Church of England (though actually made up of two provinces, those of Canterbury and York), for example, is one. A province is a national church when it is coterminous with national boundaries. It deserves the name 'national church' when it is committed to offering its ministry to the whole national community and seeks to project its message at every level of national life. The significance that Anglicans give to provinces derives from ancient catholic usage, where dioceses are gathered into provinces under a primate or metropolitan (usually an archbishop). The importance of national churches derives not only from the growing importance of national aspirations at the time of the Reformation, but also from the incarnational emphasis of Anglican theology. The incarnation represents and establishes the involvement of God with humanity in all its particularity. Anglicanism is therefore predisposed, for theological as well as historical reasons, to work with the grain of the given contours of human and social identity, expressed through geography, political structures, cultural traditions, and the shared history of a people. The role of particular or national churches has evolved within Anglicanism into an affirmation of the principle of inculturation.

⊛ Third, there is the church of the *diocese*, which is often a geographical area with a common history and sense of identity. The diocesan bishop exercises pastoral oversight within the diocese, though he usually shares his *episkope* (the New Testament Greek word for pastoral oversight) with suffragan bishops and also consults with the clergy and representative lay people, through the diocesan synod and the bishop's council, in his or her task of leading and governing the diocese. The bishop is also the president of the diocese as a eucharistic community and the chief minister of the sacraments. However, he or she shares the cure of souls and eucharistic presidency with the clergy of the diocese. It is of the essence of a diocese that the clergy and people remain in communion with their bishop. Where that communion is impaired, as it is in some Anglican dioceses over the issue of women priests, a grave anomaly has entered Anglican ecclesiology. Anglicans are perhaps beginning to realize, as a result of recent traumas over the decision to allow women to be ordained to the presbyterate (or priesthood), that they need to strengthen their sense that the diocese is also the Church of Christ. In Anglicanism, as in Roman Catholicism and Eastern Orthodoxy, the diocese, as the community united in its bishop and as the bishop's sphere of ministry, is regarded as the *local church* and this term has a technical meaning that is significant in Anglican ecclesiology.

◉ Fourth, there is the *parish*, the most local level of the Church and the smallest unit of the Church to be formally recognized by Anglicans. In the established, territorial Church of England it is the geographical parish, rather than the worshipping community itself that is recognized and there is no membership requirement to take part in the life of the church (except as far as church government is concerned, where membership of the Church Electoral Roll is required). In newer churches of the Anglican Communion, where territorial units of the Church are more of a modern administrative convenience than an ancient one, and where the congregation may tend to be even more eclectic than they are in the Church of England, Anglicans still speak of the parish as the basic unit of the Church. The church of the parish consists of a community of the baptized, together with 'catechumens' (enquirers receiving instruction leading to baptism and confirmation), and normally gathers in one place, the parish church, for worship, teaching and fellowship. Christian communities at parish level are the building blocks of the catholic Church. It is vital to grasp that Anglicans do not think of the gathered congregation as the fundamental unit of the Church, but of the diocese as the local church, comprising all the parishes within which the clergy exercise a ministry of word, sacrament and pastoral care that is commissioned and overseen by the bishop. The parish is just as much the Church as are the universal, provincial/national and diocesan manifestations of the Church.

The existence of a church, at any of these levels, can be identified, according to the Thirty-nine Articles, wherever the Word of God is preached and the sacraments of baptism and holy communion (eucharist) are administered according to Christ's institution, for these indicate that Christ is present with his people in the power of the Holy Spirit (cf. Article 19).

CATHOLICITY

In the creed, Anglicans affirm the catholicity of the Church. It is significant that they do this precisely as Anglicans, as members of, for example, the Church of England, the Church in Wales or the Episcopal Church of the USA. For in making this affirmation, Anglicans are implying that catholicism is not synonymous with Roman Catholicism. Anglicans maintain that there is a non-Roman catholicism. Catholicity refers to the universal scope of the Church as a society instituted by God in which all sorts and conditions of humanity, all races, nations and cultures, can find a welcome and a home. The catholicity of the Church denotes its potential to fulfil the aspirations of all people. Catholicity therefore points towards inculturation. It suggests that the Church has the capacity to embrace diverse ways of believing worshipping and that this diversity comes about through the 'incarnation' of Christian truth in many different cultural forms which it both critiques and affirms. Thus the catholicity of the Church, which in the past has often been a byword for authoritarianism, uniformity and the crushing of local traditions by cultural imperialism, is actually, when rightly understood, a mandate for cultural hospitality. Because the Church is essentially catholic, it cannot allow any group within its borders to feel patronized or marginalized – whether they are ethnic groups in a mainly white environment, working-class Christians in a mainly middle-class church, or women touched by the feminist critique of patriarchy in a church still largely led by men.

We now need to ask what the connection is between the catholicity of the Church and the Anglican insistence on the threefold order in historic succession. What has the historic episcopate to do with catholicity? While catholicity should not be defined solely by reference to holy order, nor reduced to it, Anglicans have maintained that ordination in the historical episcopal succession enhances and contributes to the catholicity of the Church. To take an example from the modern period, in his seminal work *The Gospel and the Catholic Church* (Ramsey, 1936), Michael Ramsey claimed that the historic episcopate was of the *esse* of the Church – essential to its very existence. Because the Church was a body, a visible society, he argued, it needed the historic episcopate to enable it to realize its true nature. The episcopate was the effective symbol of the corporate nature of the Church. Although Ramsey was remarkably affirming of traditions that lacked the historic episcopate – his work set a new standard for Anglicanism in this – he did inevitably imply that no ecclesial body which lacked it could be fully recognized as a Christian Church. However, the new ecumenical theology of communion (*koinonia*) makes it possible for Anglicans to endorse the principle that Ramsey was arguing for – the intrinsic connection between the historic episcopate and the catholicity of the Church – without appearing to unchurch other, non-episcopal communions. Let us see how this can be done.

KOINONIA

As recent ecumenical agreements – concluded between Anglicans and Protestants in the USA and Europe – demonstrate, Anglicans acknowledge a genuine *koinonia*, or fellowship with

God the Holy Trinity and with one's fellow Christians, in churches that do not have bishops in historical succession. Anglicans know that they would be deceiving themselves if they did not acknowledge the reality of *koinonia* in other churches. Those communities patently enjoy 'the grace of our Lord Jesus Christ, the love of God and the fellowship of the Holy Spirit'. Manifestly they share the faith of the Church; they have baptism and the eucharist; ministers who are commissioned by the Church and given authority to minister word and sacrament; structures of conciliarity that enable the churches to govern themselves under the guidance of the Holy Spirit; and forms of *episkope* or pastoral oversight that involve the essential biblical principle of transmitted authority.

It is the reality of *koinonia*, grounded in the foundational sacrament of baptism, that compels us to acknowledge the authenticity of the ministries and eucharists of churches that are not episcopally ordered. The steps of the theological argument can be represented as follows:

◉ Baptism unites the believer with Christ. It is, therefore, the foundation of the Christian life and the Christian ministry. The mutual recognition of baptism by most mainstream churches, the significance accorded to baptism in the Lambeth Conferences and in the Second Vatican Council, allows us to affirm baptism as the foundational sacrament of the Church, the basis and ground of all expressions of ministry. All other 'sacramental' acts (confirmation, confession/penance, the eucharist, ministerial order) are appropriations, applications or extensions of the ecclesial reality brought into being by baptism.

◉ The rationale for this primary affirmation of the significance of baptism is found in the doctrine that baptism incorporates believers into the body of Christ, the Church (1 Cor. 12.12–13), whereby they participate in Christ's threefold messianic office as prophet, priest and king. All members of this royal priesthood exercise it in a continual offering of spiritual sacrifices to God through Christ. That sacrifice is first and foremost of themselves (Rom. 12.1) and its chief expression is through the eucharist when we are united with Christ's self-oblation to the Father, caught up in the movement of his self-offering (ARCIC, 1982, p. 14).

⊚ The Church needs to set apart some members of the whole people of God (New Testament Greek: *laos*), to represent and minister to its own inherent priesthood and to reflect it back, so bringing to light the priestly nature of the whole body and of every member in particular. When the Church does this, it imparts authority for some to act in a representative – not vicarious – way on behalf of all. It is not as though baptized Christians did not already fully participate in Christ's royal priesthood. But what ordination does is to set some apart for the representative ministry as an 'economy' (a useful patristic and Orthodox term implying some temporary restriction or narrowing down for the sake of the long-term well-being of the whole) within the body. The commissioning or ordination that they receive is real, awesome and effective. When fellow ministers or bishops bestow such authority, they do so, not so much in the name of their order as in the name of the whole body of the Church and of Christ himself.

⊚ The only proper theological criterion for assessing the authenticity of a church's ordained ministry – and with it the authenticity of its sacraments, especially the eucharist – is whether it is manifestly the reflection and expression of the *koinonia* of that body, the life of communion with Christ and one another, that flows from the baptismal incorporation of all believers into Christ. Mutual recognition of baptism combines with the growing awareness of common ground in the experience of *koinonia* to create a·powerful momentum towards mutual recognition as churches of Christ with authentic ministries and sacraments. As far as Anglicans are concerned, that alone will not be sufficient for full, visible, structural unity, which represents a further stage in which the episcopate as a focus of unity and continuity must come into play, but it is the essential prerequisite for the supreme challenge of finding a basis for that ultimate step.

Such recognition has been achieved by Anglicans with the Evangelical Lutheran Church in America (ELCA) in the penultimate stage of the dialogue that has led up to the proposed 'Concordat', with the Evangelical Churches in Germany (EKD) in the Meissen Agreement and with the French Lutheran and Reformed Churches through the Reuilly Agreement (1999), as well as with the Moravian Church in Britain and Ireland. Here Anglicans have not insisted on the historic episcopate as a precondition for recognition of another church as a true church, or for practising eucharistic hospitality or even for joint celebrations (in some sense) of the eucharist, but they do continue to regard it as an essential aspect of the Church's catholicity and therefore as a prerequisite for visible unity (reconciliation). As Henry Chadwick has put it:

> *The point should not be represented as if episcopacy is the article of faith by which the church stands or falls, or as if it is the only possible instrument of unity; still less an infallible guarantee against the incidence of schism. The claim is not being made that the episcopate is of the being of the church in the sense that it is constitutive in the same way and on the same plane as the sacraments of baptism or eucharist or the true proclamation of God's Word. But unity and universality are of the church's very being ... And the episcopal ministry in due succession and apostolic commission is the immemorial tradition of the catholic church ... and therefore is also a providential instrument of the true marks of the church as a visible society in history.*

(Chadwick, 1994, pp. 87f)

Episcopal ordination in historical succession and in communion with the college of bishops of the universal Church (as far as that is possible in a divided Church) is a canonical requirement of Anglicanism and part of its distinctive discipline and polity. Moreover, Anglicans share it with the largest and most historic Christian communions: the Roman Catholic, Orthodox, Nordic and Baltic Lutheran, and Old Catholic Churches. Anglicans value it as an aspect of the catholicity and apostolicity of Anglicanism. In terms of the current ecumenical consensus, it is a sign but not a guarantee of the apostolicity and catholicity of the Church. In practice, episco-pal ordination is a non-negotiable platform of Anglicanism in ecumenical discussions, whatever temporary compromises and anomalies may be entertained in order to overcome canonical obstacles to visible unity.

APOSTOLICITY

In the Nicene-Constantinopolitan creed, Anglicans, like many other Christians, affirm also the apostolicity of the Church. The very first of the Church of England's canons asserts that it belongs to the true and apostolical Church of Christ and that no member shall be free to deny that (Canon A1). The apostolicity of the Church has been a recurring theme of recent ecumenical dialogue involving Anglicans. The churches have come to see that apostolicity is an attribute of the whole Church and stands for the momentum of the Church in mission. The Church derives its apostolicity ultimately from the mission that the Son receives from the Father and conveys to the Church, together with the gift of the Holy Spirit. '"As the Father sent me, so I send you." Then he breathed on them saying, "Receive the Holy Spirit ..."' (John 20.21–22). The Lima Statement of the Faith and Order Commission of the World Council of Churches, *Baptism, Eucharist and Ministry* (1982), defined the apostolicity of the Church in terms of its multifaceted continuity with the life of the early Christians. 'Apostolic tradition in the Church means continuity in the permanent characteristics of the Church of the apostles' (*BEM*, M34; p. 28). Apostolicity is predicated primarily of the whole body, the life in grace of the people of God. So when we speak, as we may, of an apostolic ministry, we should be clear that this is set within an equally apostolic community.

It follows from this premise of the inalienable apostolicity of the Church of Christ, that any church that is caught up in the mission of God in Christ through the Holy Spirit should be recognized as genuinely apostolic. Its ministries and sacraments are manifestations of its essential apostolicity. If it has bishops in historical succession, they serve as a sign and instrument – though not as a guarantee – of apostolicity. Historical episcopal succession, together with the ordination of presbyters by those bishops only, is a sign of God's faithfulness to the Church through history. It is also a sign of the Church's intention to remain faithful to the teaching and mission of the apostles. It assures the faithful of that intention. It is, so to speak, a sacramental link with the Church of the Apostles who were called, taught and commissioned by Jesus Christ himself and were chosen witnesses of his resurrection. It demonstrates that the Church does not feel free to cut loose from the authority of the apostolic Church, but on the contrary, believes that it is called above all to faithfulness to the gospel and to the community of the gospel with its sacraments and ministries.

However, the Porvoo agreement between the British and Irish Anglican Churches and the Nordic and Baltic Lutheran Churches has made it possible for Anglicans to take a less literalistic view of what historical succession means. These Anglican Churches have extended recognition to the episcopal succession of the Norwegian and Danish Churches, even though the succession of episcopal consecrations and ordinations was temporarily broken in the Reformation period. They have done this on three grounds, which they judge make up for that anomaly (on the principle that the Church, acting in good faith and with the right intention, has the fullness of grace to compensate for any human deficiencies, the principle of *Ecclesia supplet*). Those grounds are: first, the intention was to ordain bishops, even though they were consecrated by a presbyter (Bugenhagen); second, the succession of bishops since then has been maintained; third, there has been continuity of *episkope* (pastoral oversight) in the historic sees – a principle that was important to the early Church. In this important development of Anglican thinking about the historic succession, we see a concentration on the spirit rather than the letter: it is the intention of the Church that counts, rather than the mechanics of succession (see [Porvoo], 1993; Halliburton, 1998).

CATHOLICITY AND APOSTOLICITY

What then is the relationship between catholicity and apostolicity? The attributes of catholicity should be distinguished from those of apostolicity. Can we elicit the nature of the connection or distinction between them?

⊚ Apostolicity is the dimension of depth in the Church, its extension in time, its forward momentum in mission. Apostolicity has to do with the authenticity of the Church; its faithfulness to its apostolic foundation; the reality of the apostolic mission in the mission of the Church today.

⊚ Catholicity is the dimension of breadth in the Church, its extension in space, its aspiration to universality. Catholicity has to do with fullness and completeness; the inclusivity of the Church; the presence of the whole Church in the local churches.

Anglicans understand episcopacy in the light of both the catholicity and the apostolicity of the Church. As the Lambeth Quadrilateral suggests, Anglicans do not set the historic episcopate above the Bible, the creeds and the sacraments; it quite clearly takes fourth place after these. But it is significant that the Quadrilateral draws on both scripture and tradition. If we receive the gospel and the dominical sacraments on the authority of scripture, we also receive the canon of scripture, the ecumenical creeds and the historic episcopate from tradition. Anglicans (and for that matter, other catholic Christians who recognize the role of tradition) should not be critized because they base the claims of the historic episcopate on tradition: the canon and the creeds are also grounded purely on tradition. Non-episcopal churches that retain the canon and the creeds may be helped, by reflecting on the significance of that fact, to recognize that tradition also makes a claim upon us with regard to episcopacy.

UNITY IN BAPTISM AND EUCHARIST

Anglicans believe that unity is an inalienable attribute of the Church of Christ and that it is grounded in the trinitarian unity of the one God. For Anglicans, as Hooker taught, the indestructible unity of Christians in Christ through baptism is of the revealed essence of Christianity, for there is 'one Lord, one faith, one baptism, one God and Father of all' (Eph. 4.5). Although this unity will be fully manifested only in the last time, at the coming of the kingdom (i.e., eschatologically), the imperative of seeking to realize this God-given unity in practical, tangible, structured ways is laid upon us now by the New Testament. The unity of the Church is therefore both a divine gift and a Christian calling.

Through their commitment to the ecumenical movement, Anglicans have consistently testified that the unity of the Church, as an imperative of Christian obedience, is a condition of the Church's mission – 'that they may be one ... that the world may believe' (John 17.20–23). It is also part of God's plan for the unity of all things in heaven and earth in Christ, so that God may be all in all (Col. 1.20). By endorsing recent ecumenical insights (particularly those of *Baptism, Eucharist and Ministry*), Anglicans have indicated that they believe the Church to be a sign, instrument and foretaste of this eschatological unity. To the extent that the Church itself is divided, its effectiveness as a sign of the kingdom is impaired.

Anglicans hold that the unity of the Church is grounded in the one baptism. They have been among the first to perceive the ecumenical significance of the mutual recognition of baptism by the churches. The famous 'Appeal' for Christian unity by the Lambeth Conference of 1920 was addressed to all those throughout the world who had received Christian baptism. Baptism unites us to Christ in his death and resurrection. It incorporates us into his divinely anointed body, the

Church, and we participate in his threefold messianic office as prophet, priest and king. Baptism therefore makes all Christians into a holy, royal, priesthood. Baptism is a dynamic reality that contains an inherent drive towards deeper unity – primarily in the one eucharist – as we seek to realize together the true nature of the body of Christ.

By their practice of eucharistic hospitality, Anglicans show that they believe that the common baptism calls for unity in the eucharist – for that is where the body of Christ, to which we already belong by baptism, is most fully known. The eucharist, or holy communion, is the paradigm of *koinonia* and this concept – so fruitful in current ecumenical work – is particularly congenial to Anglicans. They have contributed to the ecumenical theology of communion and this theology is reflected particularly in the documents of the 1988 Lambeth Conference (see [Lambeth], 1988). We are already fundamentally in communion with each other through baptism (see ARCIC II, 1991), but that communion only comes to its full realization (this side of heaven) in the unity of the eucharist, the 'holy communion'. At that moment, our communion with Christ and our communion with each other are inseparable – and, perhaps, indistinguishable.

Where does eucharistic communion fit into the process of becoming more visibly united? Anglicans do not regard the achievement of a common eucharist, in its ecumenical context, as the final reward for a unity already attained in the spheres of faith and of order, as Rome and the Orthodox do. But neither do they see it as merely a pragmatic device for artificially promoting a unity that does not yet really exist. Rather, Anglicans see the eucharist as the sacrament of unity in the sense that the communion that is already a reality through our common baptism and our common baptismal faith, comes to fruition and expression there and may become more and more complete as progress in visible unity is achieved.

DIVERSITY

As members of a culturally diverse worldwide communion of churches, Anglicans are habituated to the idea that communion can coexist with considerable diversity of belief and practice. The varieties of faith and practice that are a feature of Anglicanism are held together at a fundamental level in the communion that Anglicans have with one another in the common eucharist across divisions of churchmanship (though this is currently impaired in some quarters as a result of the ordination of women as priests and bishops). That does not mean that all varieties of belief and practice are equally valid, or that the differences do not matter, or that Anglicans should not be striving for greater coherence and cohesion; only that there is something that is greater, deeper and stronger than all these differences – the fact that all the baptized belong to the one Christ and in him to one another. It is this transcendent condition of ecclesial existence that is operative in the eucharist.

The nature of the Anglican Communion, as a fellowship of churches that practise comprehension and toleration on the basis of a common core of fundamental tenets of faith and order, suggests that the model of unity that is most congenial to Anglicans is that of 'communion in diversity'. This is a good deal stronger than the familiar ecumenical expression 'reconciled diversity'. Real communion involves much more than the mutual acceptance of differences. It implies an agreed fundamental faith, a common life of sacramental worship, interchangeability of ministers, the practice of conciliarity with joint policy-making, and unity in *episkope* (however that might be worked out in practice).

Unity is focused and sustained in Anglican churches tacitly as well as explicitly. Alongside the explicit structures of common credal faith and sacramental practice, of government and oversight, there stands a common tradition that embraces liturgy, theology, spirituality and pastoral care. It is this common tradition – a distinctive Anglican ecclesial culture – that undergirds the more structural and formal safeguards

of unity such as the synods, bishops, archbishops and canon
law.

It belongs to the ethos of Anglicanism, which owes more
than is usually recognized to the pre-Reformation Conciliar
Movement in the Western Church, that its structures of unity
should be operated constitutionally and in a representative
way and in a way that acknowledges the vital consent of the
faithful. The churches of the Anglican Communion are
synodically governed and episcopally led. To put it another
way, leadership in Anglicanism is located in the bishop-in-
synod. Anglicans are averse, by tradition and conviction, to
hierarchical, monarchical and authoritarian methods of leadership and to attempts to impose a monolithic uniformity.
Anglicanism does not find a juridical approach to the unity of
the Church at all congenial. It does not typically engage in
litigation and its church courts are used only in extreme cases
of ecclesiastical discipline.

THE VISIBILITY OF THE CHURCH AND ITS UNITY

Anglicans are committed, by their tradition of ecclesiology, to
the visible expression of the Church's unity. They do not
believe that a spiritual, inward unity is enough. Article 19 of
the Thirty-nine Articles focuses entirely on the visible
Church. It defines it as 'a congregation of faithful men, in
the which the pure Word of God is preached, and the
Sacraments be duly ministered according to Christ's ordi-
nance'. There are two points that I would like to draw out
from this Article.

First, Anglicanism does not see the local worshipping
congregation as the fundamental unit of the Church. The
word 'congregation' in Article 19 almost certainly does not
mean that. The Latin text of the Article has the phrase *coetus
fidelium* (assembly of the faithful). This Article is based on
Article 7 of the Augsburg Confession of Luther's Reformation,

in which the equivalent expression is *congregatio Sanctorum* (assembly of the saints). *Coetus* is virtually a synonym for *congregatio* (assembly, society) which corresponds to the Greek *ekklesia* which we have already seen means an assembly of people. The Article is not primarily referring to what we understand by a worshipping congregation in a parish (though this is certainly not excluded, since it too must have an ecclesial integrity grounded in word and sacrament), but to a 'particular' church, which for the English Reformers meant a national church made up of dioceses. That is the flock within which word and sacrament are administered and pastoral oversight is exercised. The 'local church' in Anglican ecclesiology denotes (as we have already seen) the community of word and sacrament gathered, governed and led by the bishop. For Anglican ecclesiology, the 'congregation' in the strict sense is the diocese.

Second, contrary to a popular misconception, the churches of the Reformation – the Church of England among them – did not think of the Christian Church as essentially invisible. True, they stressed the mystery of the Church as 'hidden with Christ in God' (Col. 3.3) and there is undoubtedly an invisible dimension to Christ's Church. But the Reformers did not believe that the true Church would ever cease to exist in a visible form on earth. Thus they held the catholic doctrine of the indefectibility of the Church. Hooker spoke of the visible and 'mystical' (not invisible) aspects of the Church. It belongs to the catholicity of Anglicanism that it acknowledges the Church to be a visible, universal society, with visible, tangible structures of its common life. The unity with other churches that Anglicans seek, is therefore, certainly a visible unity. It would have to be embodied in structural, institutional forms. This concern is grounded for Anglicans in the normative model of the incarnation, which is the real visible embodiment of God in human life. The visibility of the Church, and therefore of its unity, is expressed in a number of ways: the public reading of the scriptures, the preaching of the gospel, the administration of the sacraments, pastoral care, the exercise of *episkope* and the practice of conciliarity in church government. These all entail visible, structural and institutional forms. They make us visible to each other and visible to the world (and St Paul would probably add: to the angels). Anglicans seek a unity that incorporates and works through all these various outward forms. (For an incisive critique of Article 19, see O'Donovan, 1986, pp. 88–96.)

A BLUEPRINT FOR THE CHURCH?

In its historical formularies, Anglicanism does not claim that any particular visible structures of the Church are of binding divine institution (*jure divino*). In that strict sense, Anglicans would find it difficult to maintain that there is a divine constitution for the outward ordering of the Church. Anglicans have generally assumed that ecclesiastical polity should be shaped by reason and tradition, while it should certainly not be repugnant to scripture. For example, to assert, as Hooker does, that episcopacy is of apostolic origin, is not quite the same as claiming that it is a divinely instituted and irreplaceable form of church government. Anglicans have recognized that there is a distinction to be drawn between *episkope* as such (the New Testament's term for pastoral oversight) and the historic episcopate as one expression or implementation of this – or to put it another way, between the principle of transmitted authority and the contingent historical structures through which Christ's commission is mediated to the Church and its ministers in every generation. For example, the Lambeth Conference of 1920 proposed the historic episcopate as an appropriate basis for unity precisely because it was the most widely accepted form of *episkope*. Anglicans are committed to the historic episcopate; they are wedded to it and do not feel at liberty to compromise on it.

Though Anglicanism does not claim that there is a divine constitution for the Church to be lifted from the pages of the New Testament, it does hold that certain principles of abiding validity may be discerned there. As the Ordinal shows, Anglicans believe that Christ commissioned certain of his disciples to preach the gospel, heal the afflicted, spread his teachings, forgive sins, administer the sacraments (certainly at least baptism at this stage) and care for his sheep (cf. Matt. 28.18–20; John 20.21–23). In this commission, Anglicans believe that a ministry of word and sacrament, of absolution and of effective *episkope* is entailed. The form of this *episkope* should be of the widest acceptability and provide scope for local adaptation. For Anglicans this criterion points to the threefold order of bishops, priests and deacons, and to historical continuity of ordinations by bishops.

In gladly acknowledging the apostolicity of other churches, Anglicans invite them to a mutual sharing of apostolic gifts. It is extremely unlikely that any Anglican church could be a serious partner in a scheme of visible unity that did not involve all participating churches eventually sharing in the historic episcopate. Anglicans would not be requiring this in order to make the ministries of non-episcopal churches true ministries of the word and sacraments in the Church of Christ for the first time, as though they were not that already (they recognize that as a reality by virtue of the apostolicity of the whole Church in its enjoyment of the trinitarian *koinonia* and in its apostolic mission), but it would be required in order to give effect to the visible unity of the Church through the effective sign of apostolicity, the historic episcopate.

UNIVERSALITY

For Anglicans, the visibility of the Church should come to expression at each of the various levels of the Church:

- in the parish, through one eucharistic fellowship in each place with an episcopally ordained president;
- in the diocese ('local church'), through the one bishop acting in council with his or her assistant bishops, together with the priests, deacons and lay persons, in one synod;
- provincially or nationally, through a united college of bishops

and a synod in which bishops, clergy and laity are represented;

⊙ internationally or globally, through appropriate structures of consultation, discernment and decision-making (conciliarity) with a president accepted by all.

That final point raises the question of the office of a universal primacy. The principle of a primacy wider than the province or national church is not alien to Anglicanism. The Archbishop of Canterbury has a primacy in the Anglican Communion, though he remains first among equals (*primus inter pares*) (see Podmore in Podmore (ed.), 1998). Anglicans have not excluded the possibility in principle of a universal primate. The statements on authority of the ARCIC *Final Report*, which not surprisingly suggested that the Bishop of Rome would be a suitable candidate for universal primate in a united church, was acknowledged as a useful contribution to ongoing discussion by the 1988 Lambeth Conference and the bishops of the Church of England gave a cordial but not uncritical response to the Pope's encyclical *Ut Unum Sint* of 1994. The idea of an Anglican 'reception' (evaluation, critical assimilation) of papal primacy has once again been raised in a fairly sharp form by the ARCIC report *The Gift of Authority* (ARCIC II, 1999).

In any consideration of universal primacy, Anglicans would want to stand firm on their foundational principles (which go back to the Conciliar Movement of the fourteenth and fifteenth centuries) of dispersed authority, constitutional constraints on authority, the principle of consent, and representative synods that include elected lay people and clergy other than bishops. To speculate whether, on those terms, agreement on primacy could be reached with the Roman Catholic Church where the pope has universal immediate jurisdiction, power of infallible utterance and a veto in councils of bishops and requires implicit obedience to his routine teaching in faith and morals, is beyond the scope of this brief introduction to the Anglican understanding of the Church of Christ.

Select Bibliography

Works cited in the text, together with suggestions for further reading.

ARCIC (Anglican–Roman Catholic International Commission), 1982. *The Final Report*, London: Catholic Truth Society/SPCK.

ARCIC II, 1991. *Church as Communion*, London: Catholic Truth Society/Church House Publishing.

ARCIC II, 1999. *The Gift of Authority*, London: Anglican Communion Office.

Archbishops' Group on the Episcopate, 1990. *Episcopal Ministry*, London: Church House Publishing.

Avis, P., 1982. *The Church in the Theology of the Reformers*, London: Marshall, Morgan and Scott.

Avis, P., 1986. *Ecumenical Theology and the Elusiveness of Doctrine*, London: SPCK; Cambridge MA: Cowley Press (as *Truth Beyond Words*).

Avis, P., 1989a. *Anglicanism and the Christian Church: Theological Resources in Historical Perspective*, Edinburgh: T. & T. Clark; Minneapolis: Augsburg/Fortress Press.

Avis, P., 1989b. *Eros and the Sacred*, London: SPCK.

Avis, P. D. L., 1990. *Christians in Communion*, London: Geoffrey Chapman Mowbray; Collegeville: Liturgical Press.

Avis, P., 1992. *Authority, Leadership and Conflict in the Church*, London: Mowbray; New York: Trinity Press International.

Avis, P., 1996. 'Keeping faith with Anglicanism' in Hannaford (ed.), 1996.

Avis, P., 1998a. 'Anglican conciliarity and the Lambeth Conference', *Theology*, vol. CI, no. 802 (July/August 1998), pp. 245–52.

Avis, P., 1998b. 'The distinctiveness of Anglicanism' in Podmore (ed.), 1998.

Avis, P., 1998c. 'What is Anglicanism?' in Sykes, Booty and Knight (eds), 1998.

Avis, P., 1999. *Anglican Orders and the Priesting of Women*, London: Darton, Longman & Todd (Affirming Catholicism series).

Baptism, Eucharist and Ministry, Geneva: WCC, 1982.

Board of Mission and Unity, 1986. *The Priesthood of the Ordained Ministry*, London: Church House Publishing.

Bradshaw, T., 1992. *The Olive Branch: An Evangelical Anglican Doctrine of the Church*, Carlisle: Paternoster Press.

Bray, G., 1998. *The Anglican Canons 1517–1947*, Boydell Press and Church of England Records Society.

Carlton, C., 1987. *Archbishop William Laud*, London: Routledge.

Chadwick, H., 1994. *Tradition and Exploration*, Norwich: Canterbury Press.

Chadwick, H., 1995. 'Anglican ecclesiology and its challenges', *One in Christ*, 31 (1995), pp. 32–41.

Coleman, R. (ed.), 1992. *Resolutions of the Twelve Lambeth Conferences 1867–1988*, Toronto: Anglican Book Centre.

Churches Together in England (CTE), 1996. *Called To Be One*, London: CTE.

Doctrine Commission, 1995. *The Mystery of Salvation*, London: Church House Publishing.

Doe, N., 1996. *The Legal Framework of the Church of England*, Oxford: Clarendon Press.

Doe, N., 1998. *Canon Law in the Anglican Communion*, Oxford: Clarendon Press.

Figgis, J. N., 1922. *The Divine Right of Kings*, Cambridge: Cambridge University Press, 2nd edn.

General Synod of the Church of England, 1994. *Apostolicity and Succession*, London: Church House Publishing (House of Bishops Occasional Paper: GS Misc 432).

Gilley, S., 1990. *Newman and His Age*, London: Darton, Longman & Todd.

Gore, C., 1884. *Roman Catholic Claims*, London: Longmans, Green & Co.

Griffiss, J. E., 1997. *The Anglican Vision*, Cambridge MA: Cowley.

Groupe des Dombes, 1993. *For the Conversion of the Churches*, Geneva: WCC.

Guiver, G., 1990. *Faith in Momentum*, London: SPCK.

Halliburton, J., 1998. 'Bishops together in mission and ministry: the understanding of episcopacy in the Porvoo Common Statement', *Theology*, vol CI, no. 802 (July/August 1998), pp. 253–62.

Hannaford, R. (ed.), 1996. *The Future of Anglicanism*, Leominster: Gracewing.

Hill, C. and Yarnold, E. (eds), 1994. *Anglicans and Roman Catholics: The Search for Unity*, London: SPCK/Catholic Truth Society.

Holeton, D. (ed.), 1996. *Renewing the Anglican Eucharist*, Cambridge: Grove Books.

Hooker, R., 1845. *Works*, ed. J. Keble, Oxford: Oxford University Press.

House of Bishops of the Church of England, 1997a. *Eucharistic Presidency*, London: Church House Publishing.

House of Bishops of the Church of England, 1997b. *May They All Be One*, London: Church House Publishing.

House of Bishops of the Church of England, 2000. *Bishops in Communion: Collegiality in the Service of the Koinonia of the Church*, London: Church House Publishing.

Jacob, W. M., 1997. *The Making of the Anglican Church Worldwide*, London: SPCK.

Kaye, B., 1995. *A Church Without Walls: Being Anglican in Australia*, Victoria: Dove.

[Lambeth], 1988. *The Truth Shall Set You Free*, London: ACC/Church House Publishing.

McGrath, A. E., 1998. *The SPCK Handbook of Anglican Theologians*, London: SPCK.

Macquarrie, J., 1997. *A Guide to the Sacraments*, London: SCM Press.

Maurice, F. D., 1958. *The Kingdom of Christ*, 2 vols, ed. A. Vidler, London: SCM Press.

More, P. E. and Cross, F. L. (eds), 1935. *Anglicanism: The Thought and Practice of the Church of England, Illustrated from the Religious Literature of the Seventeenth Century*, London: SPCK.

Newman, J. H., 1974. *An Essay on the Development of Christian Doctrine*, Harmondsworth: Penguin.

O'Donovan, O., 1986. *On the Thirty-nine Articles*, Carlisle: Paternoster Press.

Percy, M., 1999. *Introducing Richard Hooker and the Laws of Ecclesiastical Polity*, London: Darton, Longman & Todd (Affirming Catholicism series).

Platten, S., 1997. *Augustine's Legacy: Authority and Leadership in the Anglican Communion*, London: Darton, Longman & Todd.

Podmore, C. (ed.), 1998. *Community – Unity – Communion: Essays in Honour of Mary Tanner*, London: Church House Publishing.

[Porvoo], 1993. *Together in Mission and Ministry*, London: Church House Publishing.

Rahner, K., 1961–. *Theological Investigations* (23 vols), London: Darton, Longman & Todd; Baltimore: Helicon Press/New York: Crossroad.

Ramsey, A. M., 1936. *The Gospel and the Catholic Church*, London: Longmans, Green and Co.

[Reuilly], 1999. *Called to Witness and Service: The Reuilly Common Statement with Essays on Church, Eucharist and Ministry*, London: Church House Publishing.

Sachs, W. L., 1993. *The Transformation of Anglicanism: From State Church to Global Communion*, Cambridge: Cambridge University Press.

Sykes, S. W., 1984. *The Identity of Christianity*, London: SPCK.

Sykes, S. W., 1994. 'Foundations of an Anglican ecclesiology' in J. John (ed.), 1994, *Living the Mystery*, London: Darton, Longman & Todd, pp. 28–48. Also in Sykes, 1994, pp. 122–9.

Sykes, S. W., 1988. 'Anglicanism and the Anglican doctrine of the Church' in J. R. Wright (ed.), *Quadrilateral at One Hundred* [Anglican Theological Review Supplement], Cincinnati: Forward Movement Publications; London: Mowbray, pp. 156–77. Also in Sykes, 1994, pp. 101–21.

Sykes, S. W., 1994. *Unashamed Anglicanism*, London: Darton, Longman & Todd.

Sykes, S. W., Booty, J. and Knight, J. (eds), 1998. *The Study of Anglicanism*, London: SPCK; Minneapolis: Fortress Press.

Thomas, P. H. E., 1998. 'Doctrine of the Church', in Sykes, Booty and Knight, 1998, pp. 219–31.

Vogel, A. A. (ed.), 1984. *Theology in Anglicanism*, Wilton CT: Morehouse Barlow.

Walker, P., 1988. *Rediscovering the Middle Way*, London and Oxford: Mowbray.

Wright, J. R., 1990. 'Prolegomena to a study of Anglican ecclesiology' in Armentrout, D. S. (ed.), *This Sacred History*, Cambridge, MA: Cowley, pp. 243–56.

Index